CW00820478

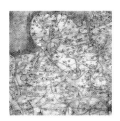

The Gough Map

The Gough Map

The earliest road map of Great Britain?

NICK MILLEA

BODLEIAN LIBRARY
UNIVERSITY OF OXFORD

TREASURES FROM THE BODLEIAN LIBRARY

The Bodleian Library, founded in 1602, is the principal library of the University of Oxford and one of the world's great libraries. Over the past four hundred years, the Library has built up an outstanding collection of manuscripts and rare books which make up part of our common cultural heritage. Each title in this lavishly-illustrated series, Treasures from the Bodleian Library, explores the intellectual and artistic value of a single witness of human achievement, within the covers of one book. Overall, the series aims to promote knowledge and to contribute to our understanding and enjoyment of the Library's collections across a range of disciplines and subjects.

First published in 2007 by the Bodleian Library
Broad Street, Oxford OX1 3BG

www.bodleianbookshop.co.uk

ISBN: 1 85124 022 5
ISBN 13: 978 1 85124 022 7

Design and typeset by Baseline Arts, Ltd
Series design by Dot Little
Typeset in Monotype Centaur
Printed and bound by South Sea International Press, China
British Library Catalogue in Publishing Data
A CIP record of this publication is available from the British Library

Contents

ortes dant tholom̄ salus ie li enuoi
ngtrer me porra premerain el tornoi
i messages respont volentiers par ma for
i portiers lor desferme la porte du grauoi

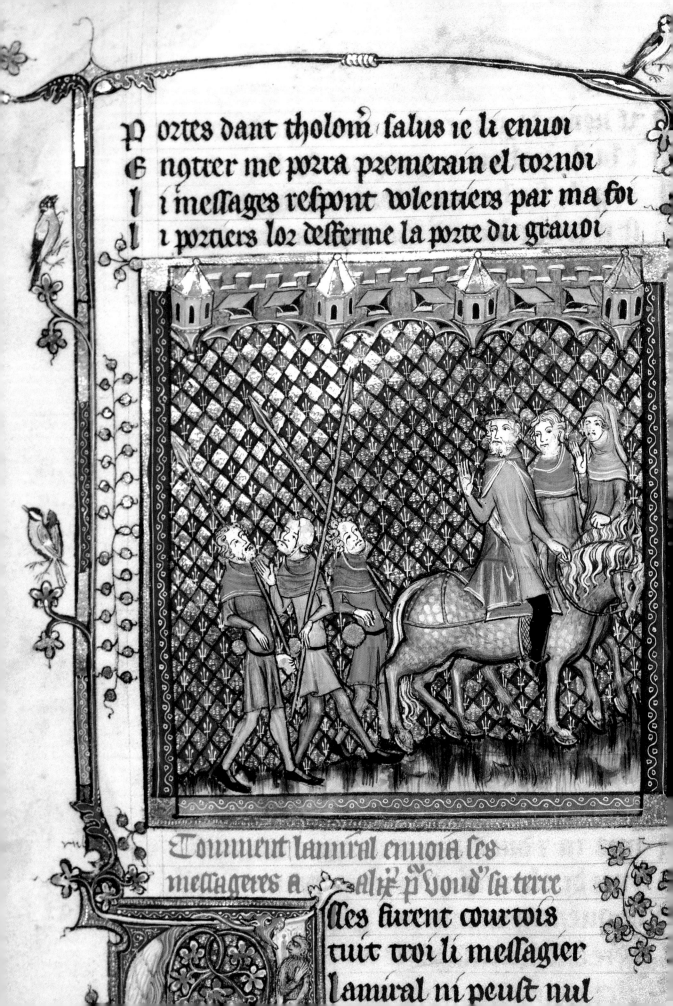

Coument lamiral enuoia ses
messageres a   Alix̄ p̄ voud̄ sa terre
lles furent courtois
tuit troi li messagier
lamiral ni peust nul

Preface

The Gough Map, held in the Bodleian Library, University of Oxford, is an enigma. It depicts the geography of medieval Britain in unparalleled detail, but despite the wealth of information it conveys, very little is known of its creation, its purpose and its audience. We now have an opportunity to explore more of the map's message and methodology as a result of new imagery which has recently been made available.

Two catalysts have brought this book about. The first was the realisation that the Bodleian Library's reprint of E.J.S. Parsons' *The Map of Great Britain circa AD 1360*[1] had itself fallen out of print. This book is very much a reworking of Parsons' classic, from which much of the original text has been retained and reproduced, particularly in Chapters Five, Six and Eight. The appendix is a rearrangement of Parsons' alphabetical listing of the Gough Map's towns into geographical subdivisions.

The second catalyst was the imagery captured by DigiData Technologies Limited[2] on 4 June 2004 as part of a project entitled *The Gough Map – Gateway to medieval Britain* for the Oxford Digital Library,[3] financed by the Andrew W. Mellon Foundation[4] as one of a series of Development Fund initiatives taking place in 2004/2005.[5] This has furnished researchers with a further chance to take a look at the map itself, and allowed us to illustrate the map in far greater detail than before, adding clarity and helping to bring fourteenth-century Britain to life. The imagery will now be made freely available via the Oxford Digital Library, enabling the reader of this book to examine at first hand the cartographic intricacies identified within the body of the text. Rob Watts, formerly of DigiData Technologies, has provided the detail for the relevant section of Chapter Eight, based on his well-received presentation to The Oxford Seminars in Cartography on 2 June 2005.[6]

A major (and coincidental) advance occurred during the late summer of 2004, when the author was contacted by Professor Bruce Campbell of Queen's University Belfast requesting permission to capture the Gough Map digitally. Campbell and his team from Queen's were applying for British Academy[7] funding for a research project, using geographical information systems (GIS), entitled *Mapping the Realm: English cartographic*

FIGURE 1
Illustration from a decorated copy of *The Romances of Alexander,* Oxford, Bodleian Library. MS. Bodley 264, 83v.

construction of fourteenth-century Britain.[8] Funding was subsequently awarded, the Bodleian supplied the imagery, and by mid-2005 a working website was in place. More details on *Mapping the Realm* appear at the end of the book.

In Wallis's *Historians' guide to early British maps*, Paul Harvey describes the Gough Map as 'The most remarkable cartographic monument of medieval England'.[9] It has long generated considerable interest in the academic community and beyond, and it is hoped that this volume will pose further questions surrounding the map's origins and purpose, in turn encouraging additional research and study.

A Most Curious
and Ancient Map

I N *Richard III*, John of Gaunt famously describes England as *This precious stone set in a silver sea*. For modern theatre-goers, the shape of that precious stone is easy to picture: the outline of the country, from the tapering leg of Cornwall in the west to the jutting bulk of East Anglia in the east, is familiar to us from thousands of maps and atlases. But in the fourteenth century, when Gaunt lived, to be able to look at even a vaguely accurate depiction of it was a novelty. The few of his contemporaries in a position to do so would have been highly educated: an ordinary person, shown a two-dimensional representation of his homeland, would not have had the first notion what it was. Furthermore, this élite would in all probability have derived its knowledge from a single document – the Gough Map, which has survived for six and a half centuries to become one of the great treasures of the Bodleian Library.

This remarkable artefact is the earliest surviving map to show routes across Britain, and to depict it with a recognisable coastline. There is no record of any similar contemporary map at such scale or indeed accuracy:[10] such is its quality and detail that it remained the blueprint for cartographers for 200 years.

Measuring 55.3 by 116.4 cm (or just under two feet by four),[11] it is drawn on two pieces of animal hide which were originally sewn together, though the stitching has long since disappeared. The larger piece contains three-quarters of the map, with the join (which is remarkably straight) running through the middle of Scotland, just below Loch Tay. No scale is given, but it can be calculated at close to 1:1,000,000, or sixteen miles to one inch.

The dominant colours are white, for the land, and green for the sea and rivers. Although the map is generally very well preserved,[12] the green – once much brighter – has faded with time to a pale wash stained with some darker blotches. This fading is particularly noticeable at the bottom of the map: the result, perhaps, of past users leaning on the edge as they pored over it.

But there is another important colour, surviving as a bolder pigment: red, which has been used for the majority of the map's inland features – most prominently, for hundreds of tiny drawings of houses, castles and churches representing centres of population. Red is also used for river names (written in a careful and elegant script), and for a series of straight lines which join many, but not all, of the 600-odd settlements, with figures in Roman numerals (indicating distances) written against each line. The positioning of the names and figures, and the orientation of the symbols, mean that the map is directed towards the east (rather than the north, as modern maps are). In this it follows the convention of earlier maps, presenting a theocentric view of the world, which were oriented towards the holy city of Jerusalem.

Although the map is, to our eyes, instantly recognisable, some parts are much more accurate than others. The east and south coasts are particularly well delineated, as is the area around York. (London and York are given much larger vignettes than anywhere else, and had their names written in gold.) Wales, on the other hand, lacks one of its most prominent features – the great inlet of Cardigan Bay; while Scotland tails off into a landmass of almost uniform width, rounded at the northern end.

Another characteristic of the map is the prominence given to rivers, extending to the sea like the root system of a tree. Each has its source represented by a circular node, and each is disproportionately wide, in the same way that the blue lines representing motorways are exaggerated in scale on today's road maps. Other natural features such as hills and mountains are occasionally included, though there are a handful of forests – for which the mapmaker's symbol is a pair of intertwined trees – and of lakes.

Off the mainland lie several dozen islands, of which the most important – including the Isle of Wight, the Isle of Man, Anglesey and the Channel Islands – are named and given vignettes to indicate settlements. Here again the degree of accuracy varies: the Orkneys (then under the rule of Norway) are represented as one large island with three (non-existent) rivers, to the east rather than the north of Scotland – though it could be that its position was dictated by the space available on the vellum.

The edges of two further landmasses frame the map: to the west, Ireland, and to the east a vague amalgam of Scandinavia and continental Europe,[15] running from Norway through Denmark ('Dacia') and Flanders to France. A number of place names appear on each: in Ireland *Stranford* (Strangford), *Carlenford* (Carlingford), *Drowdaa* (Drogheda) and *Develyn* (Dublin); in Scandinavia and the Continent, *Norway, Dacia* (Denmark), *Sklus* (Sluis), *Graveling* (Gravelines), *Caleys* (Calais), *Whitsand* (Wissant), and *Boleyne* (Boulogne). There is also one castellated vignette representing Calais – the King of England's foothold in France from 1347. Sluis' presence could be attributed to Edward III's great naval victory of 1340, when his defeat of Philip VI of France's navy at the Battle of Sluis marked the opening encounter of the Hundred Years War.

In addition to place names, the map holds a variety of written information. In England eight county names are given: four in the south-east (*Essex, Kant, Norfolk and Suffolk*) and four in the south-west (*Cornubia, devonia, dorset and Somerset*). It is difficult to explain why only these eight were included, for there is no evidence that any others have disappeared with time: it may be that the name of the county town in some cases was considered sufficient. There are also a number of interesting district names, such as *Aundernes* (Amounderness) in Lancashire. *Arderne* (Arden) in Warwickshire could refer to a forest or a district, and *albus equus* in Berkshire to the Vale of the White Horse or (less probably) the actual figure of the horse.

The map – which takes its name from Richard Gough, an eighteenth-century antiquary and authority on British topography – is a thing of beauty, in which the almost abstract forms created by the rivers' tentacles are counterpointed by the fastidious delicacy of the mapmaker's vignettes and script. But it is also a thing of mystery. (It was described at the sale in which Gough bought it as 'most curious and ancient'.) Although it depicts the geography of the age to an unparalleled level of detail, we do not know who commissioned it, created it or used it; nor do we know its purpose (was it a map for travellers, or something more?) or exactly how its network of red lines works. The fact about it that we can most nearly ascertain is its date – but even this is more complicated than it at first seems.

Two features of the map deepen the mystery: an inscription referring to popular mythology, and a series of drawings. The inscription – positioned off the coast of Devon near Dartmouth – reads *hic Brutus applicuit cum Troianis* ('here Brutus landed with the Trojans'). The significance of this purported settlement of Britain by a descendant of Aeneas is something we will return to later in the book.

Of the drawings, the largest is of a ship with a broken mast, possibly caught on rocks between Orkney and Norway. Next to it are two rafts – one also on the rocks, the other in the sea. Sanders originally speculated as to their precise meaning, and other commentators suggested various interpretations as to what may, or may not be represented on the map.[14] Lying on the seaborne raft is a stretched-out figure with long hair, wearing a loose-fitting garment belted at the waist with a cord or rope. Beyond this is the outline of another drawing, either obliterated or never completed, of a figure in a second boat.

Meanwhile, farther away in the middle of the ocean, a group of sea creatures swims: one a swordfish, the other two less identifiable. The arrangement of the fish suggests that they could be fighting, and it has been suggested, again by Sanders, that the largest figure is that of a whale confronting its two natural enemies the swordfish and the thrasher (or fox-shark). But did the mapmaker include them simply for decoration, or with a symbolic purpose? It is questions like these that make the Gough Map not only the most detailed and accurate depiction of Great Britain from the medieval period, but also the most enigmatic.

Edward I and Empire

GIVEN THE NUMBER of questions surrounding the Gough Map, it is remarkable that its creation can be dated to within eleven years. The earliest possible date is 1355, the year in which work started on the town walls of Coventry, which are shown on the map;[15] the latest is 1366, when Sheppey (as it is called by the mapmaker) changed its name to Queenborough in honour of Queen Philippa, Edward III's wife.[16]

But to say that the map was made in the mid-fourteenth century is not to say that it was *designed* at that time. In fact, there is much to suggest that what the Bodleian possesses is an updated copy of an older map, conceived in the reign of Edward I (1272-1307) rather than that of Edward III (1327-1377) and possibly drawn up as early as 1280.[17] Within this period of 70-odd years, Britain – and indeed the whole of Europe – was transformed by the greatest catastrophe of the Middle Ages, the Black Death, which reached England in 1348 and ultimately killed 40 per cent of the population; but there appears to be no reference to this upheaval in the map's content.[18]

It has been argued that there could have been several copies made of the original,[19] held in different parts of the country and adapted with the help of the users' local knowledge: according to this theory, the Gough Map would have been kept somewhere in Lincolnshire or south-east Yorkshire, explaining the fact that it shows a particularly intricate network of red routes for that area.[20] To commission a copy of the map would not have been a difficult thing in an age when the reproduction of any document had to be done by hand; but every copy made would create opportunities for mistakes to creep in, and the existence of two of these on the Bodleian version suggests that it is not original. The mountain of Plynlimon in central Wales should – according to the map's use of symbols – be represented by a cogged wheel, but here a circle has been erroneously filled in, giving it the appearance of a lake.[21] An identical mistake has been made with Dartmoor.

The idea that the map's prototype was made under Edward I is based on some strange emphases in it – particularly concerning Wales. Although the network of red lines shows two major routes going into Wales from England, neither is the obvious one for a traveller to take, either in the Middle Ages or the present day. One runs along the north and west coast from Chester to

Cardigan, creating very much an encircling impression; the other, further south, leads from London to St David's, crossing the border in the vicinity of Clyro. As this route progresses westwards it deviates from its expected course (that of the modern A40) by avoiding Llandovery: instead, it makes a turn at Trecastle (near Sennybridge) and goes through the mountains to reach the Towy valley at or near Llangadog.

Only when the history of Edward I's wars against the Welsh is considered does the significance of these routes become clear. In 1277, following his successful first campaign against Llywelyn ap Gruffudd, Edward gave orders for new castles to be built on the coast at Flint, Rhuddlan and Aberystwyth (as well as one inland at Builth). After the suppression of the Welsh revolt of 1282-1283, further castles were added at Caernarvon, Conway and Harlech, while the captured Criccieth Castle was rebuilt. In 1283-1284 a road was constructed to link these four with the other coastal castles – and it is this which the map's northerly route follows.[22] The southerly one, meanwhile, is that taken by the King's army in order to put down a further rebellion in 1295.[23] In addition, it should be noted that Snowdon is one of the few mountains identified on the map, possibly because it was also a military stronghold for the Welsh forces.

If all this is indicative of how well Edward I's armies knew Wales, the lack of detail at the north end of the map shows how little they knew Scotland – at least until the end of his reign. Not only is the outline of the country completely inaccurate, but very few towns are identified: instead, the names given tend to be those of earldoms. (An examination of these supports the theory that the Gough Map is based on an earlier document:[24] although the Earldom of Buchan, which is shown, existed in 1280, it had become dormant by the mid-fourteenth century.[25]) Nor are there any routes marked. Had the map been designed in Edward III's time, one would expect a much greater degree of accuracy, since by then the English had conducted several large campaigns against the Scots. But in the late thirteenth century Scotland was still very much a foreign country to any mapmaker south of the border – one whose size and internal geography had to be guessed at. It was only in 1296 that Edward I, having concentrated his expansionist efforts in Wales, began to wage war there.

Was the Gough Map, then, conceived as a military map? The answer to this – and to the question of whether it is a conventional road map – is very likely to be no, for the simple reason that it does not include some of the major thoroughfares of the day. There is no route shown, for example, from London to Dover (the modern A2), and few of the well-known Roman roads are featured.

Instead, we seem to be dealing with a geopolitical map which presents the country in the light of Edward I's achievements – a statement, as it were, of its condition and extent. In the words of Daniel Birkholz, author of *The*

King's two maps: cartography and culture in thirteenth-century England, the map asserts that Britain is 'a single monarchy of the whole island, unified under the king of England', with the route from Chester to Cardigan representing 'a military chain each of whose links connotes…an English conqueror's secure rein upon Wales'.[26]

Birkholz makes a connection between the map and the survey known as the 'Little Domesday' project initiated by Edward in 1279. In March of that year, the King appointed panels of commissioners to 'go personally to all and singular places' in every English county 'so that all the towns, hamlets, and other tenures shall be written in books, to be delivered to the King by the commissioners'. In doing so, he mentioned a 'desire to redress the state of his realm'. The results for only a few counties survive (known as the Hundred Rolls, they cover Oxfordshire, Cambridgeshire, Huntingdonshire, and – in part – Berkshire and Warwickshire), so it is not possible to say how successful the survey proved; but it may very well be that some of the information gathered was used in compiling the map.

There are no borders or boundaries shown on the map, giving the impression that it represents a single administrative domain. It is, Birkholz argues 'a map to engage the imagination of early English imperial travellers, especially the aristocratic and clerical élites backing Edward I's aims of overlordship in Britain'. This suggests that it was made for (and indeed by) agents of an expanding English empire, and Birkholz interprets it as illustrating 'the acquisition of territory.'

Unfortunately, Birkholz's suggestion of possible royal involvement is not (as he readily accepts) supported by evidence from any surviving contemporary documents. However, we do know of royal interest in maps in the reign of Henry III (1216-1272), when the idea of kingship was strongly linked to territorial statehood: indeed, a change was made to the King's coronation vows to include a clause 'whereby the King promised not to alienate rights and possessions of the Crown and to recover what had been lost'.[27] The significance of this addition was not lost on Edward I, who referred to this extra undertaking on at least eight occasions during his reign as a means to validate his expansionist intentions into Wales and then Scotland.

It is possible, then, to see the Gough Map in part as an early form of propaganda – a view supported, as we shall see, by a study of its mythological references.

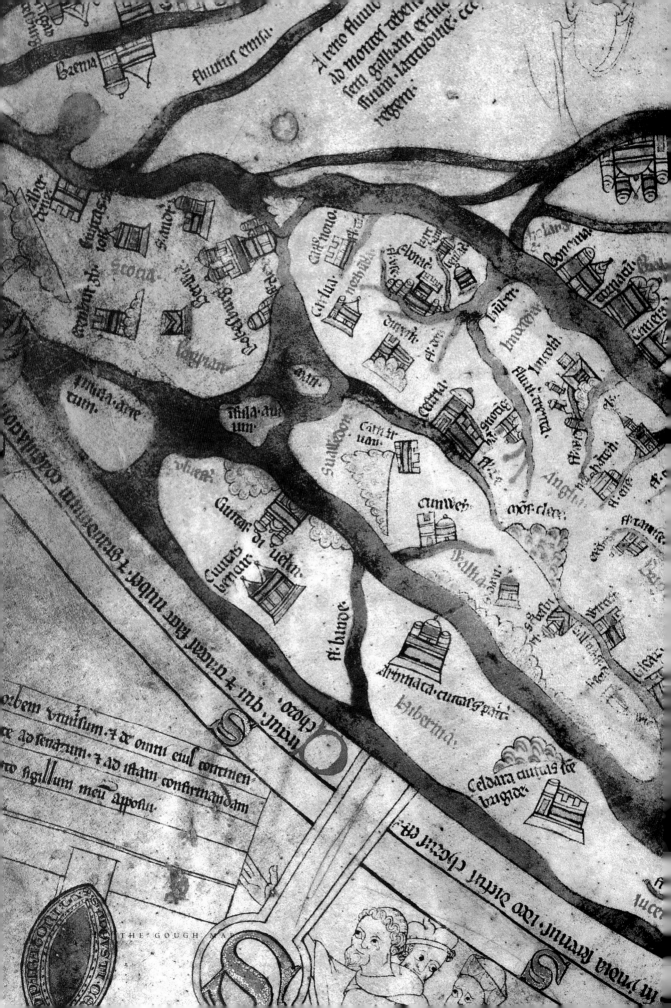

A Revolution in Mapmaking

To APPRECIATE the importance of the Gough Map fully, it is necessary to understand what kind of maps existed before it, and how people found their way from one place to another without the kind of information it supplies.

Although earlier maps depicted space, they did not do so in a way that was of any great use to travellers, being as much concerned with heaven as they were with Earth. As Evelyn Edson and Emilie Savage-Smith put it in their book *Medieval views of the Cosmos*, 'Maps in early medieval Christendom, particularly World maps, were attempts to explore theological and historical aspects of space, rather than to make scale models of the physical world'.[28]

The Hereford *Mappa Mundi* is a particularly interesting example, since it dates from approximately the same time as the prototype Gough Map. It is a theological interpretation of the World, created in around 1285 for an audience fully cognisant of Christian tradition and teaching. Jerusalem is placed at the centre of the map, and around it revolves the World, depicted both in spatial form and in temporal form. East is at the top, with the Garden of Eden representing the beginning of time, while flowing westwards through the map there is a general temporal movement towards the late thirteenth century.

Not only is the scale too small to be of practical use, but the representation of Britain is crude compared to that of the Gough Map. England is approximately an elongated oval; Wales is roughly differentiated from it, but there is no indication of the south-western peninsula of England, and the east and south coasts are very nearly in one line, facing the Continent. The outline of Scotland is dictated by the trend of the continental coasts and the frame of the map; in addition, it is almost entirely severed from England. The sole realistic elements are the rivers and a number of towns.

Even in Edward III's reign there were mapmakers working in this tradition, apparently without regard for advances in practical cartography. An example is Ranulf Higden of Cheshire, who produced a map of the

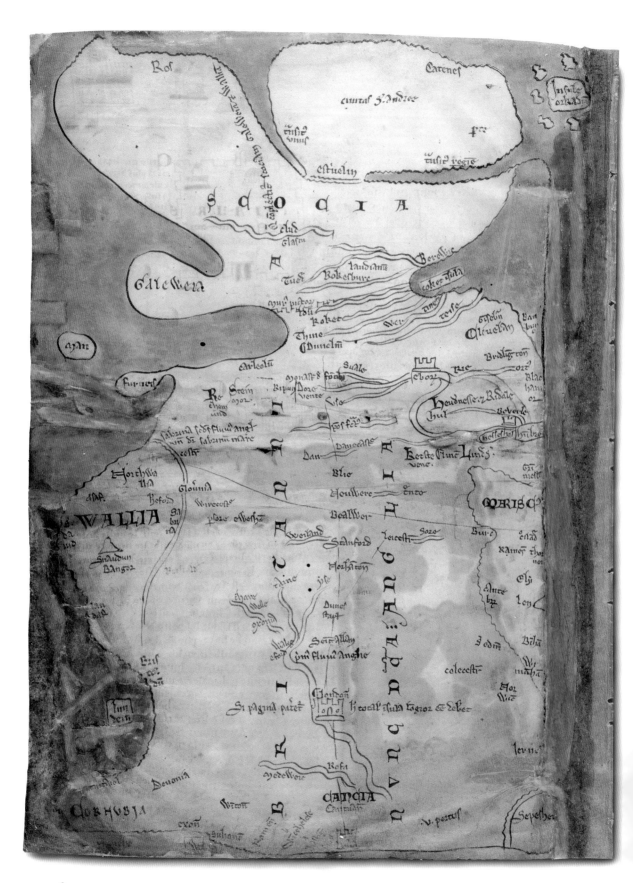

FIGURE 3 (previous spread)
A close up of Great Britain from
the *Mappa Mundi* held at Hereford
Cathedral.

FIGURE 4
Matthew Paris *Map of Britain*
British Library. MS Royal 14. C. vii,
fol.5v.

World before his death in 1363 which is centred on Jerusalem and features Adam and Eve in Paradise. Whether he did not know of the Gough Map, or simply chose to ignore it, we cannot say for certain, but he shows England as no more than a small rectangular label in the ocean, stating 'Anglia' alongside 'Wallia'.[29]

Apart from placing east at the top, and featuring cathedrals and monasteries, the Gough Map shows very little theological input (though Daniel Birkholz argues that it nevertheless 'builds on the visual, cultural and epistemological traditions activated by ecclesiastical *mappae mundi*',[30] changing the emphasis and to make a political — as opposed to theological — statement). Instead, it is a map showing an actual landscape: a concept alien to most of the mapmaker's contemporaries. The royal court could have been able to make use of it, as well as a number of Government administrators, monasteries and other places of learning — but scarcely anyone else.

What, then, did travellers rely on before maps as we know them came into use? The answer in the Middle Ages, as in Roman times, was itineraries: i.e. lists giving the sequential names of places which must be travelled through in order to arrive at a destination, and the distances between them. (One of the most famous of these, the Peutinger Table — a medieval copy of a Roman document — has some stylistic similarities to the Gough Map, including the use of vignettes to represent towns, and Roman numerals to show distances.) Ironically, the development of computer technology has revived this approach to journeys, with drivers relying increasingly on itineraries downloaded from motoring websites, or serial instructions given by satellite navigation systems in their cars.

Many medieval itineraries were devised for the benefit of pilgrims, and are geographically extensive in their scope, outlining journeys to Rome or even Jerusalem. Their disadvantage was their rigidity: they catered only for those following established routes, and any deviation from them was hazardous, since signposts were not yet a feature of the countryside and the user could not be sure of picking up the prescribed path again. Not that this inherent design flaw has ever been considered unduly problematical — Ogilby enhanced such an approach in the seventeenth century,[31] and motoring organizations have seen no reason to deviate from this proven wayfinding method into the twenty-first century.

Among the itineraries surviving from the Middle Ages are several of journeys made by Edward I and Edward III, which demonstrate further surprising omissions from the Gough Map, since some of the commonly used routes they followed are not included on it: for example, that from York to Newcastle. This route does, however, feature in four versions of a map of Britain produced in around 1250 by one of the leading historians and cartographers of the day, Matthew Paris.[32]

A Benedictine monk based at the monastery of St Albans, Paris was responsible for at least fifteen maps, including a *mappa mundi*, a map of Palestine and an itinerary to the Holy Land. His maps are far from possessing the accuracy of the Gough Map, but they are elaborate pieces of work, and they place a strong emphasis on roads, including Roman ones such as the Fosse Way, the Icknield Way and Watling Street. The most interesting of the British group, the map in *Cotton MS Julius D.vii, fol. 49v*, shows a rudimentary peninsula in the south-west of England; Wales is differentiated after a fashion (its general outline is not unlike that of the Gough Map), but it is placed far to the north of its true position, extending from opposite King's Lynn to opposite Durham. The east and south coasts are poorly rendered. The other maps do nothing to improve the representation, except one (*Cotton MS Claudius D.vi, fol. 12v*) on which the outline of north Norfolk is emerging. So far as Scotland is concerned certain features suggest a common, though remote, origin with the Gough Map.

Curiously, Paris' procedure seems to have been to construct the topography of his map around itineraries, rather than vice-versa. His chief axis is the pilgrim route from Newcastle upon Tyne to Dover (possibly extending even further north to Berwick-upon-Tweed),[33] which is shown as a straight line in the centre of the map, with the lie of the land adjusted to fit in with this.

But land maps were not the only precursors to the Gough Map: the invention of the magnetic compass in the late twelfth or early thirteenth century had greatly helped the development of sea charts, which were far in advance of their terrestrial equivalents. Known as portolans, these were – in the words of Evelyn Edson and Emilie Savage-Smith – the first European maps 'based on the faithful rendering of travelled space';[34] the oldest surviving one dates from 1275, and some of those drawn for Mediterranean sailors included Britain.[35] The fact that the Gough Map is the first map to show the country with a relatively recognisable coastline has led to suggestions that it may have been based on such charts[36] – particularly with regard to the south and south-east coasts, the Bristol Channel and the North Sea. If this was the case, then it could be that the outline of the country was constructed first, and that the inland topography (which was unlikely to be of relevance to seamen, and therefore not included in the portolans) was added afterwards.[37]

The problem with the portolan theory is that there are some very important coastal features which appear on charts of the time but are not included on the Gough Map.[38] Prime examples are The Lizard and Start Point – both essential for the mariner, yet completely ignored by the mapmaker.[39] The characteristic features of a portolan – such as loxodromic (direction) lines radiating from wind roses, and place names closely written at right-angles to the coast – are also missing.

The Gough Map, moreover, shows a broad-brush approach to the coastline: a maritime cartographer, paying close attention to bays and headlands, would have given it a far more jagged appearance. Nor is it likely that he would have made the cardinal error of omitting Cardigan Bay.

Whichever of these possible antecedents the mapmaker drew on, all were developed for purposes which made them of very limited help to the general traveller. The Gough Map represents an enormous leap forward, presenting geographical information in a form which was both much more efficient and (once the idea of it was grasped) usable by a much larger group of people. Who its users may actually have been, we will examine in the next chapter.

A l'entrer des herberges truevent ·i· latimier
Et demandent le tref alixand d'alier
Seignoz bien le vous sai respont cal enseignier
Ves le la ce plus haut a ce pomel d'omier
Jel ui ores monter sus vairon son destrier
Par le mien enscient vait soi esbanoier
E parler voles vous naues qua targier
I message s'entoznent pensent de l'esploitier
Ngtrent alixand sous l'ombre d'un lozier
Cil diex qui forma terre ⁊ adam le premier
De la coste adam fist euain sa moillier
Gariffe l'amiral ⁊ fi doint encombrier
A tous ceuls qui a tort le vuelent guerroier
Uant fait il il le vous mande ne vous doit anuier
Por iffir de sa terre vous donra bon loier
Plus or ne porteroient ·xxiiij· sommier
Se nel voles prendre a celer ne vous quier
Lamiral vous deffie ⁊ tuit fi chevalier

The Map's Audience

JOURNEYING THROUGH BRITAIN in the Middle Ages was not easy. For one thing, the road system was poor, and little was done to try to improve it. No major highways were constructed between the time of the Roman occupation and the turnpike era more than 1,300 years later, and of the roads that were built, few benefited from any kind of formal engineering. The continued dependence on an ancient infrastructure is illustrated by the fact that, of the routes depicted on the Gough Map, around 40 per cent of the total mileage follows the course of known Roman roads.

The roads were, moreover, badly defined and maintained. What is now the A30 across Salisbury Plain was in places a mile wide, while others consisted of no more than boggy tracks through woods, which travellers negotiated – in the absence of road signs and maps – by making their way from one clearing in the trees to the next. So heavily forested was the countryside that on Edward I's Welsh campaigns up to 1,800 woodcutters went ahead of his army to make a passable route for it.[40] For this reason heavy goods tended to be transported by sea or river – hence the prominence given to rivers on the Gough Map.

For the great majority of people there was, in any case, little opportunity or reason to travel. Peasants were tied to the land, and had to work it hard to meet their obligations. As for their families and friends, these would in all probability live in the same village, so visiting them seldom involved a journey. The poor were also limited to the distance they could travel on foot, since only the affluent possessed horses.

Those who did travel on a regular basis included merchants, pilgrims, lawyers, soldiers, members of religious orders and royal couriers and commissioners. It could be, then, that the Gough Map was designed for one of these specific groups.

But as we have seen, while it was far in advance of any other cartographical aids, there were limits to its usefulness for anyone planning a journey. Not only are some major routes missing, but also many natural obstacles such as areas of high ground. It is therefore worth examining the possibility that it was commissioned with an administrative purpose in mind,[41] either by the Church or by the State.[42] As Evelyn Edson and Emilie Savage-

Smith note in *Medieval views of the Cosmos*, 'Travellers generally did not make use of maps in the Middle Ages, but sought the advice of local guides or joined groups going in the same direction, such as the pilgrims in The Canterbury Tales…Even the marine charts seem to have been used originally by businessmen and administrators at home, and only occasionally taken to sea.'[43]

Matthew Paris's maps prove that the expertise to create the Gough Map could have been found in a monastery; but there is nothing in its content to suggest that it was made for ecclesiastical purposes. Although York had its name lettered in gold, this does not seem to be connected with its status as an archbishop's seat, since the same honour was not accorded to Canterbury; and while churches with spires feature among the vignettes, these vignettes are predominantly secular.

A much more likely possibility is that the map was produced for use by servants of the Crown. As Catherine Delano-Smith and Roger Kain have observed, in thirteenth-century Britain 'the total population moved towards a peak unprecedented since Roman times (with perhaps 4 to 5 million people by 1300)…and as record-keeping became more important, so maps began to be more widely used as practical tools.'[44]

If the map does indeed assert the establishment of an empire, as suggested in Chapter Two, then the ability to administer that empire was of no less importance than the conquest of new territory. Taxes could not be raised if the Government did not know where the King's subjects were to be found, or have an idea of their wealth. The statistical data sought in the Little Domesday survey would have been enormously valuable in this respect, but for the twenty-first-century observer, putting it to good use would be unthinkable without maps. (Around 80% of all information collected in Britain today has some geographic element.[45]) The idea that the Bodleian's map was a working document, adapted from an older prototype and updated with local information as it was gathered, fits in well with Crown-servant theory.

But what evidence is there that the Gough Map was employed for this purpose? Intriguingly, it has been conjectured that a version of the map was in use in 1324-1325, when Robert of Nottingham was buying wheat for Edward II in the East Midlands. According to records of the Exchequer Accounts,[46] Robert cites identical distances to those included on the map: the question is whether he had seen the Gough Map (or more applicably a prototype of it), or whether the map's compiler employed distances between towns that were already familiar to the medieval traveller.

Further circumstantial evidence can be found in the map's later history, leading up to its acquisition by the Bodleian.

The map came to the Library in 1809 as part of a bequest made by Richard Gough, consisting of a magnificent collection of books and maps.[47] (It was at this point that it became known as 'the Gough Map'.) Gough himself had bought it for half-a-crown on 20 May 1774 at a sale of part of the collections of Thomas Martin of Palgrave, a Fellow of the Society of Antiquaries: offered as lot 405, it was described as 'a curious and most ancient Map of Great Britain'.[48] (The lot number is still fixed to the back of the map.)

The minute book of the Society of Antiquaries tells us that Thomas Martin had shown the map there on 5 May 1768. The entry, which is the earliest known reference to the map, reads: 'Mr T. Martin exhibited a very antient MSS. Map, on Vellum of Great Britain, in wch London & York are distinguished with Letters of Gold. He deems it to be about the Age of K. Edward 3rd.'[49] (As Martin was an expert palaeographer who 'had the happiest use of his pen, copying, as well as tracing, with dispatch and exactness, the different writing of every aera', this lends further weight to the theory of the map's date advanced above; his opinion was supported by other palaeographers who examined the map in the mid-twentieth-century.[50])

It is doubtful whether Martin gave to the Fellows who attended the meeting any information as to how the map came into his possession, for if he had it is fairly certain that Gough would have repeated it in his book *British topography*.[51] But there is a strong possibility that he acquired it through his friendship with Peter Le Neve, a passionate collector who became Norroy King-of-arms and the first President of the Society of Antiquaries. Martin had known Le Neve since boyhood through their common interest in topography and antiquities, and was appointed his executor.

Le Neve's collection of books and manuscripts was extensive and important. The sale of his library in February and March 1731, two years after his death, lasted for twelve days: among the lots were more than 2,000 printed books and 1,250 manuscripts. Thomas Martin bought a great many of the documents, and soon afterwards married Le Neve's widow, by whom he came into possession of a further very valuable collection of English antiquities and pictures.

Le Neve had amassed many early maps (he had even contemplated making additions to William Camden's *Britannia*, the first comprehensive geographical and historical study of Britain, published in 1586); so it is reasonable to speculate that Martin found the Gough Map among them. When we consider that Le Neve had been a Deputy Chamberlain of the Exchequer (an office which he held until 1705-1706), we have a link with a Government department which theoretically could originally have used and even commissioned the Gough Map. By Le Neve's time, the map had long been superseded by others, and would probably have been regarded by the Government as an obsolete document which could be sold – or even given away – to an interested antiquary.

The Thin Red Lines

THE MOST PERPLEXING feature of the Gough Map is the network of thin red lines linking settlements, with their accompanying numerical values. If the map is ever to be understood fully, the true significance of these must first be established. Do they represent actual roads? Gough himself certainly thought so, writing that 'the greatest merit of this map is, that it may justly boast itself the first among us wherein the roads and distances are laid down'[52] – but again we come back to the question of why certain principal routes in existence at the time of the map's creation have been omitted. Furthermore, hundreds of the settlements shown do not have any lines connecting to them at all. (It is not as if the Gough Map shows a token selection of routes: the network's length amounts to around of 2,940 miles or 4,727 kilometres.)

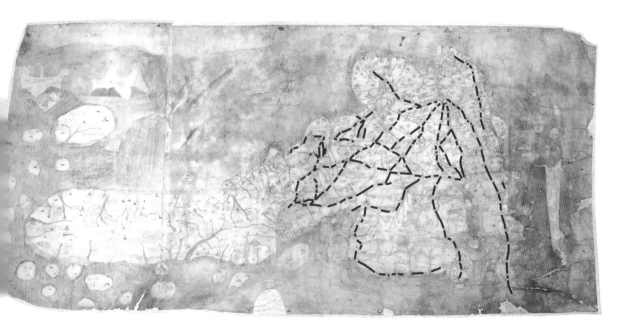

FIGURES 6 and 7
Queen's University Belfast image with routes marked compared to detail
of the thin red lines on the original Gough Map, Bodleian Library,
University of Oxford. MS. Gough Gen. Top 16.

Having said that, some of the lines do form extended patterns which spread across the country, suggestive of long-distance routes that a traveller might follow. The five principal ones radiate from London and join it with East Anglia, south Wales, and south-west, central and north-west England; secondary ones join Bristol and Worcester with north, north-west, and central England. There are also traces of a link between Bristol and the south – a route being shown to Axbridge and one possibly to Wells. In the south, a coastal route is shown from Southampton to Canterbury, and part of a westerly one from Bridport to Lyme. In Wales, the coastal route discussed in Chapter Two is shown running from Cardigan to Caernarvon and then through Bangor to join the Bristol-Liverpool route at Chester. Six local routes are shown radiating from Lincoln and another six from York.

And yet York – the second most important city on the map after London – is poorly served by main routes: it is only linked to the rest of the network by a north-westerly one at Leeming, whereupon it joins the London to Carlisle via Stainmore route. Lincoln, meanwhile, was the country's seventh most populated borough in 1348, but the web of local routes in which it is enmeshed is totally unconnected and does not extend beyond the confines of Lincolnshire.[53] If we consider the other most populated boroughs for that year, we find that neither Plymouth (fifth), King's Lynn (ninth) nor Colchester (tenth) are linked into the route system.

Similarly, London is not linked to the south coast, with the exception of a far from direct south-westerly route to Exeter. The route mentioned from Southampton to Canterbury takes in Havant, Chichester, Arundel, Bramber, Lewes, Boreham Street, Battle, Winchelsea, Rye and Appledore, but at no point does it connect to the capital. To compound the mystery, the very well-known London-Dover route does not appear, although its key stopping points (Gravesend, Rochester, Sittingbourne, Faversham and Canterbury) are all included, as is a bridge over the Medway at Rochester. The same is true of London to Ipswich (Brentwood, Chelmsford, Witham, Colchester and Cattawade Bridge are marked as settlements), and from York to Newcastle upon Tyne (Thirsk, Northallerton, Croft, Darlington, Durham, Chester-le-Street are all marked).

Named roads such as the Fosse Way, the Icknield Way, and even part of Watling Street are also omitted, despite all three featuring heavily in Matthew Paris' work. There are no routes shown in Cornwall or Scotland (and indeed north of Hadrian's Wall), and as previously mentioned, only two in Wales, one from Chester to Cardigan, and the other from London to St David's.

Nevertheless, in the words of Sir Frank Stenton, 'Whatever the limitations of his knowledge, the compiler of the map had at least arrived at the conception of a national system of roads radiating from the national capital.'[54] This may seem obvious today, but was not to Matthew Paris, who showed the 'Four roads of England' converging around Dunstable.

Of Gough's five main routes, the one from London to Exeter runs through Kingston, Cobham, Guildford, Farnham, Alton, Alresford, Winchester, Salisbury, Shaftesbury, Sherborne, Crewkerne, Chard and Honiton; from Exeter it continues via Okehampton, Camelford, Bodmin and St Columb to St Ives. A second route goes from London to Bristol through Brentford, Colnbrook, Maidenhead, Reading, Newbury, Hungerford, Marlborough and Chippenham.

The unusual nature of the route from London to south Wales has been discussed in Chapter Two. The English section runs via Uxbridge, High Wycombe and Tetsworth to Oxford, then on to Witney, Burford, Northleach and Gloucester, before passing through Newent, Hereford and Clyro to Brecon. Three smaller branches come off it at Oxford, one going to Abingdon; one linking up with the Exeter route mentioned above at Reading; and another to Bristol through Faringdon and Malmesbury.

Another of the principal routes runs from London to Carlisle, and is notable for having two smaller routes which cut across it. The first is at Coventry, which is reached by way of Barnet, St Albans, Dunstable, Stony Stratford, Buckingham, Towcester and Daventry. The detour via Buckingham is another of the map's mysteries, since it ignores a far more obvious way along an established Roman road from Stony Stratford to Daventry. (Stony Stratford is also the starting point for a branch of the route going through Northampton and Market Harborough to Leicester.)

The route which crosses at Coventry runs from Worcester to Grantham via Droitwich, Solihull, Coventry, Leicester and Melton Mowbray. The main route continues north-westwards through Coleshill and Lichfield, where it meets the second cross-route (also running from Droitwich via Birmingham, Derby, Chesterfield and on to Doncaster). From there it pursues its way through Stone, Newcastle-under-Lyme, Warrington, Wigan, Preston, Lancaster, Kendal, Shap and Penrith before ending in Carlisle.

The fifth and last of the principal routes begins, as Sir Frank Stenton pointed out in his paper *The Roads of the Gough Map*,[55] by following the course of the Old North Road, through Waltham Cross to Ware and then Royston, Caxton and Huntingdon. The next settlement it links is Ogerston, which no longer exists but was once a property belonging to the Knights Templar (Edward I stayed there in 1299 and 1303). From there it runs to Wansford and then broadly follows the route of what is now the A1 through Stamford, Grantham, Newark and Tuxford. After Blyth it reaches Doncaster, which is also the beginning of a secondary route to Wakefield, Bradford, Skipton, Settle and Kirkby Lonsdale (where the road splits, one branch leading to Kendal, the other to Shap). The main route continues to Pontefract, Wetherby, Boroughbridge, Leeming, Gilling, Bowes, Brough, Appleby and finally Penrith, where it meets the London-Carlisle route.

THE BISHOP=RICKE OF DVRLAM
AND CVMBERLAND, WESTMORELAND,
YORKE=SHIRE, LANCAST=SHIRE, AND
PARTE OF LINCONSHIRE

The Scale of Myles

FIGURE 8
Jenner's road map of Britain
2nd folio (Cumberland, etc.)
Bodleian Library, University of
Oxford. Wood 466, fol 2.

But whereas these principal routes make sinuous progress across the country, it should be noted that the thin red lines which constitute them are uniformly straight, in a way that the majority of roads are not. When we consider the Roman numerals which can be found (also in red) beside each of these lines, it looks very much as if they are in fact graphic devices to indicate distances, rather than representations of existing highways.

What unit of measurement is being used on the Gough Map is not clear, though it is somewhere between ten and eleven furlongs.[56] One possibility is that it is the old French mile, which is approximately equivalent to two kilometres.[57] (The English mile of 1,760 yards was not standardised until the publication of John Ogilby's atlas *Britannia* in 1675.) The distances seem to be 'crow-flight' distances, and agree in most cases with corresponding distances implicit on the maps produced by Christopher Saxton in the reign of Elizabeth I; those for routes known to have been used for royal visits are notably more accurate than others.[58]

The Gough Map is in fact the earliest surviving map to combine routes with distances, adding to its great significance. Such a combination was not repeated in British cartography until 1671, when Thomas Jenner issued his map *The kingdome of England & principality of Wales exactly described* … – occasionally referred to as 'The Quartermaster's map' – which appeared on six sheets at a scale of around 1:380,000. (It was reissued in 1676 by John Garrett with additional roads taken from Ogilby's *Britannia*.)

That the measurement of distance is essential to the mystery of the red lines is supported by the fact that nowhere do they appear without an accompanying numeral. It seems that to the mapmaker's mind, two settlements could not be linked unless he could establish how far they were apart. This may be seen as a qualification to the statement of empire discussed in Chapter Two, for only where the King's administration was firmly established could such facts confidently be ascertained – which would explain why all of Scotland (and most of Wales) is without red lines.

It is possible that the answer to the enigma was once spelt out in the lower right-hand corner of the map – the position where one would expect to find details of its purpose, along with its compiler's name and date of compilation – for traces can be seen there of several lines of writing. But, frustratingly, with the passage of time they have become indecipherable.

Symbols and Inscriptions

I N THIS CHAPTER we will consider the other symbols essential to the working of the map, and some of the accompanying inscriptions. We will then look at their combined effect by concentrating on one area, modern Oxfordshire, as defined by the post-1974 local government boundaries.

SETTLEMENTS

Artistically, the vignettes for cities, towns and smaller settlements are the most striking of the Gough Map's symbols. They are formed by images which fall into six basic groups: lone houses; lone houses with spires; multiple houses; multiple houses with spires; town walls; and castles.[59] The vignettes vary in overall grandeur, with the towns at the bottom of the scale each represented by a single building simple in design, while those at the top feature a combination of an imposing church with spire, a tower, a crenellated wall, and often a house or two. London is particularly splendid, with windows and a portcullis picked out in silver leaf, and its name – like York's – in gold lettering; the remaining towns are identified in a more functional black/brown.

Do the symbols represent the town's status? Some authors, including Parsons, suggest they do, whilst others disagree. There are 40 walled towns, for example, and in terms of attention to detail the most impressive vignettes (other than London and York) appear to be Berwick, Bristol, Canterbury, Carlisle, Durham, Gloucester, Lincoln, Ludlow, Newcastle upon Tyne, Norwich, Nottingham and Rochester.[60]

As a general rule, cathedral cities and monasteries are identified by crossed spires, whilst military sites are shown with towers and/or crenellations. But unfortunately the imagery created for the larger towns does not appear to be characterised by accurately selecting existing buildings and placing them in their correct location: instead, the buildings tend to be of a standard design, placed randomly within the urban landscape. So the towns in England look similar in appearance to their recently-acquired (Welsh) or foreign (Scottish) counterparts, using similar building symbols. (The five walled towns in Wales are Cardigan, Conway, Haverfordwest, Presteigne and Radnor.) Since other medieval maps with cities often include unique local detail, Daniel Birkholz speculates that this standardisation was a means of showing that all cities in Britain were the same under the King. The only overseas city to warrant a vignette, Calais (which became part of the English realm in 1347), is presented in the same style.

There are many combinations of symbols. High Wycombe, for example, is shown with two simple buildings; Oakham as a church or single building with a tower; Preston as a church with spire; King's Lynn as a church with spire and two single buildings. Some vignettes are of castles only – for example Windsor (which is very well drawn), Brecon and Castleton.

There is no doubt that originally every symbol and every river on the map had a name, though many in Cornwall, Devon, Somerset, Wales, Scotland, and the islands have faded or been rubbed off with use, with the result that not all the settlements on the map can be identified. The surviving names for most of them are written in English, though some of the more important ones are in Latin (such as *Eboriens* for York), as is all the lengthier text on the map and the names of some other features such as seas and mountains.

Many names have been overwritten in a later hand, which in some cases has made them difficult to read, though in others both forms are clearly visible. Perhaps the most striking example is the double naming of Lewes in Sussex, which features on the map as both Lewes and Lewis. This supports the theory that the map was regularly updated according to the knowledge gleaned by clerks in the place where it was held.

Similarly, a number of symbols have been inked over: this can be seen in the spires of Chelmsford, Dartford, Leicester, Lewes, Shoreham and Winchester. It is almost impossible to say when this overwriting was done.

RIVERS

Rivers are the Gough Map's lifeblood. Numerous and conspicuous (as on many medieval maps), they flow vein-like across it, occupying a considerable area and conveying the impression that they are a fundamental part of the design. Except to the north of Hadrian's Wall and away from the coast, they are depicted with a solid dark outline; by contrast, the pattern of red lines appears almost as an afterthought. The relatively widely spaced double lines with which they are drawn depict them as far wider than they are in reality; they also tend to be the same width right across the map, so that a river rising in the hills may be given the same prominence as the Mersey Estuary.

The comparison has already been made between this and Ordnance Survey's use of its blue motorway symbol – which also occupies a far greater an area than it should – on small- and medium-scale mapping of Great Britain. In terms of transportation, the river was indisputably medieval England's counterpart to the twenty-first-century motorway, and the waterways' prominence can be considered key to the map's overall function. As an over-wide motorway is shown to dominate the landscape on maps unashamedly designed for motorists, so the Gough Map's rivers appear to assume an equally powerful presence. Crossing points are very rare: although there is a bridge crossing the Medway at Rochester, it has no route to accompany it.

The rivers have circular heads, illustrating the medieval idea that all rivers had their sources in lakes. Every river of significance is included, and their positions are indicated with fair accuracy, at least in England – though since they are generally represented as being nearly straight or only slightly curved, their courses are characterless. (Among the rare exceptions are the circular watercourses which surround inland islands, such as the Isle of Axholme in Lincolnshire and the Isle of Ely to the north of Cambridge.) Some have errors of direction near their sources, but this is generally to avoid entanglement with the headwaters of neighbouring rivers. The Thames, for example, does not show the northern loop between Windsor and Reading, nor the one upon which Oxford stands, whereas its chief tributaries are well represented. The main elements of the Trent system are delineated (though with minor inaccuracies, such as showing the Dove as flowing into the Derwent), and the same appreciation of the general pattern is shown in the Great Ouse, the Yorkshire Ouse and the Severn.

The River Wear at Durham is most unusual, in that the map's compiler was clearly well aware of the local geography, showing the dramatic horseshoe curve around the castle and cathedral in great detail. Nowhere else is there such a pronounced adherence to geographical accuracy, although the scale of the Wear's course on the map is grossly exaggerated. What is certain, however, is that the map embodies a considerable knowledge of the English river system – a knowledge which could only have been accumulated over a great many years.

LAKES

There are three confirmed lakes shown on the map. They appear as circles with wavy lines best seen on Loch Tay in central Scotland. The other two lakes are Windermere in the English Lake District, and the nearby Tarn Wadling (formerly the Wathelan) – a small lake of Arthurian legend, now drained and cultivated, with clues to its current location and former identity given only in its name and the hollow it occupies in the landscape.

Authors have argued for further lakes in south-west Scotland and in the Pennines close to Bradford,[61] but these symbols appear to represent an inland island and Peak Cavern (marked *Puteus Pek*) respectively. The latter is a curious circular feature with what appears to be a tree at its centre.

HILLS AND MOUNTAINS

In contrast to the map's rivers, the compiler has paid little attention to mountains, perhaps because they hindered rather than assisted communications, or perhaps because they would encumber the map and make it more difficult to read. The only high ground shown in central or southern England is Bodmin Moor and Dartmoor, and in northern England the Cheviot Hills and the Cumbrian Mountains of the Lake District. Attention is called to the Peak in Derbyshire, but this is to the caverns there rather than to the high ground. In Wales, only Snowdon and Plynlimon are shown and named.

The north of Scotland includes numerous unnamed mountains, which seem to show an appreciation of the location of the Grampians, though they are shown running across the country from west to east. One range north-east of Loch Tay and west of Arbroath could be the mountains of Breadalbane; another group just to the north probably includes Ben Nevis and Creag Meaghaidh. The only other mountains shown further south are *lomond mons* near Loch Leven and *Mons Crofel* (Mount Criffell).

The symbols for mountains generally resemble cogged wheels, the best example being Snowdon. Similar symbols are used for the Cheviots and the Cumbrian Mountains, while the more formidable mountain ranges in Wales and that in northern Scotland are represented by long 'scalloped' bars very similar to those on the Hereford *Mappa Mundi* and common in medieval cartography.

FORESTS

Three symbols of two intertwining trees can be found on the map, representing the New Forest, Sherwood Forest, and an unnamed forest on the Isle of Bute. Other forests are named but are not accompanied by the tree symbol. The Forest of Dean and Inglewood Forest are marked in red text surrounded by red borders, whilst Arden is similarly named, but not in the context of a forest — it is shown solely as a region. It has been suggested by Daniel Birkholz that the forests with the tree symbol were given it because of their status as royal hunting forests; but the forest on Bute was not royal, while Wychwood (which was) is not included.

HADRIAN'S WALL

This is one of the Gough Map's most pronounced features, reflecting the dominant impact it must have had on the landscape before parts of it were dismantled (particularly in the eighteenth and nineteenth centuries, to provide building materials for farm walls). It is depicted on the map as a red crenellated wall, running in an unbroken straight line across northern England, and labelled with its popular name *murus pictorum* ('the Picts'

Wall'). Its positioning is not entirely accurate: it extends too far to the east, reaching to the North Sea at Tynemouth (rather than inland at Wallsend), and in the opposite direction terminates on the wrong side of the River Eden. It does, however, cross the River North Tyne in the correct place.

ANIMALS

Two animals appear on the map – a deer and a wolf, both in Scotland. The wolf is positioned in Sutherland, and the deer in Gaick Forest north of Loch Tay. Their function may be partly decorative, occupying otherwise blank locations on the map; or they may represent wild, unknown country, well beyond the bounds of England. However, the deer is accompanied by the words *Colgarth hic maxima venacio* ('Colwyth: excellent hunting here')[62] and the wolf by the inscription *hic habundant lupi* ('wolves live here'), which suggests at least a degree of local knowledge.

INSCRIPTIONS AND REGIONAL FEATURES

The Gough Map contains a number of other inscriptions describing places. Some of these are placed within cartouches, others not. One of the most curious of them, concerning Brutus's landing in Devon, will be discussed in the next chapter. Also much debated, however, is the phrase *Hic fit sal* ('Salt is made here') written in red to the right of the town symbol for Droitwich in Worcestershire. This brief economic commentary makes the settlement unique and is an important factor in the map's overall message, making clear Droitwich's significance in medieval England. The presence of salt might not have been essential information for the traveller of the day, but for merchants involved in commerce, this was a vital addition. (Daniel Birkholz also notes the importance of salt as a food preservative for an army on the march.)[63] In terms of the route network, Droitwich lies on the line from Bristol to Grantham, and is the starting point for a further route heading north-east via Birmingham and eventually to Doncaster. This, and the River Salwarpe (*fluvius salw...*), makes it a minor hub.

Other statements on the southern portion of the map include a description of the size of Anglesey as 24 miles in longitude and 18 in latitude (*Insula de Anglesey habens xxiiij mil. in long, et xviij in lat*). Ultra-violet light has revealed a further inscription on a label in the sea west of Motland (now St George's Island or Looe Island), near Liskeard – unfortunately it is indecipherable except for the consecutive letters *magna*.

In Scotland, there is a peculiar inscription by Loch Tay, attributing to it three wonders – a floating island, fish without intestines, and a passage without wind (*'in isto lacu tria mirabilia insula natans pisces sine intestinis fretum sine vento'*). According to Richard Gough, these features were commonly attributed by Scottish authors to Loch Lomond, with which Loch Tay had possibly been confused. Birkholz takes it as evidence that the map's compiler was reduced to relying on the 'geography of hearsay' in his treatment of Scotland and the Scottish Marches.[62]

Two parts of Scotland – the Earldom of Buchan and Kincardineshire – have references to mountain passes, which seem to run through the Grampians: one is that from Glen Clova to Glen Muick (*Month capell hic unum passagium*), the other Cowie Month (*Monthe colli hic unum passagium*). In Perthshire, at the junction of the Forth and Teith, there is also a mention of a *passagium*, this time a ford – that at Drip (*hic passagium de drippes*). To the west of Lanark are the words *locus dictus polcorum*, which could be translated as 'area called place of the pools'. Arbroath has the inscription *fundatur in honore sancti Thome Cant*, referring to the abbey founded in 1178 by William, King of Scotland and dedicated to St Thomas Becket.

In Wales, off the coast of Caernarvonshire, Bardsey Island is shown with the words *Bardesey ubi sunt britonum vaticinatores* ('Bardsey where the soothsayers of the Britons are'). This is despite the fact that the bards were largely suppressed by Edward I after his conquest of the country. Glamorgan has two descriptive labels: *Plaga dicta Glamorgan* ('place called Glamorgan') and *Wallia australis dicta venedocia* ('southern Wales called Venedocia').

OXFORDSHIRE

We can now combine a number of these symbols and inscriptions into one geographical area by concentrating on that part of south-central England occupied by twenty-first-century Oxfordshire. (This is an area considerably larger than the Oxfordshire described in the Appendix, since Parsons' gazetteer was initially published sixteen years before the local government boundary changes of 1974, when a significant proportion of Berkshire was transferred to its more northerly neighbour.) The four categories of symbol to be found here are settlements, routes, rivers and regional inscriptions. Each of these will be examined independently.

Settlements

Twelve towns (or villages) are included on the map: Abingdon, Banbury, Burford, Chipping Norton, Faringdon, Middleton Stoney, Oxford, Tetsworth, Thame, Wallingford, Witney and Woodstock. Of these, seven are linked by the route network, whilst Banbury, Chipping Norton, Middleton Stoney, Thame and Woodstock remain isolated. Wallingford is notable in that it is incorrectly positioned on the east bank of the Thames.

Of particular interest are the symbols used to depict these places, which are largely adorned with roofs coloured red. Oxford has a grand vignette featuring the castle and a spired church, with the possibility of four smaller buildings and a town wall. Abingdon is portrayed with a tall spired church

FIGURE 9
An enlargement of the Gough Map depicting Oxfordshire settlements, routes and rivers, Bodleian Library, University of Oxford. MS. Gough Gen. Top. 16.

topped with a cross situated behind two small buildings. Banbury and Wallingford both have a castle tower placed to the right of a single building. The remaining eight settlements are all represented by a stand-alone building made up of a gable end with a single opening, and a frontage, usually with two openings.

Routes

Four routes are indicated on the map, depicted – here as elsewhere – as straight, thin red lines linking towns, and accompanied by a red figure in Roman numerals indicating the distance between the two locations. They follow the directions of the modern A40 (Burford–Witney–Oxford–Tetsworth), the Gough Map's St David's to London route; the A420 (Faringdon–Oxford), a branch of the Bristol to London route; the A4183 (Oxford–Abingdon), which is merely a branch off the main network; and the A4074 (Oxford–Wallingford), on a route linking Oxford and Reading.[65]

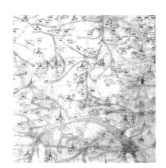

Rivers

The rivers Cherwell, Evenlode, Thame, Thames and Windrush feature prominently on the map. There is also an unidentified river that bisects Chipping Norton and Woodstock and flows into the Windrush to the north of Witney. No such river exists in reality, as the local topography would require it to flow uphill. As with the rest of the map, all rivers are shaded green within a pair of dark bounding lines, and all the Oxfordshire rivers flow out of small bulbous circles. River width is largely consistent within the county, so the Thames looks to be as broad as the Evenlode, which is clearly not the case on the ground.

Inscriptions and regional features

Such features are relatively uncommon on the map overall, except for a number of Scottish earldoms, and the preponderance of regional names where the route network is at its most dense – that is, south-east Yorkshire and Lincolnshire. Just one regional feature can be found in Oxfordshire, the Vale of White Horse, written in red in an enclosed box as *albus equus*.

Myths and Images

ALTHOUGH THE ILLUSTRATIONS in the North Sea, and the Brutus reference off the south Devon coast form a relatively small proportion of the map, much speculation on their identity, purpose and meaning has been discussed by commentators, and this chapter is very much a compilation of interpretations of what may (or may not) have been the intention of the map's creator.[66]

The use of legend – particularly Arthurian legend – is an intriguing addition on what appears to be a map depicting geographical fact. There are four Arthurian locations labelled on the map: Glastonbury in Somerset, where Arthur was reputedly buried; Pendragon Castle in Westmorland, said to have been built by his father King Uther Pendragon; Tintagel in Cornwall, traditionally Arthur's fortress; and the Wathelan, the lake between Carlisle and Penrith mentioned in the previous chapter. The Wathelan (drained in the late nineteenth century, and the area now named Tarn Wadling) features in two fifteenth-century Arthurian romances as 'a magical lake of transformative powers',[67] and its presence on the map can only be a direct consequence of its links with Arthur, since it was otherwise of little consequence.

A second legend is also given major significance on the map. The south Devon coast is shown as the landing place of Brutus, the great-grandson of Aeneas, and a group of Trojan exiles who had been enslaved in Greece. The faint text in a roughly rectangular box opposite Dartmouth reads *hic Brutus applicuit cum Troiani*.

The opening stanza of the anonymous poem *Sir Gawain and the Green Knight*, also dating from the fourteenth century, sets the historical scene for this legend:

SIÞEN þe sege and þe assaut watz sesed at Troye,
Þe borȝ brittened and brent to brondeȝ and askez,
Þe tulk þat þe trammes of tresoun þer wroȝt
Watz tried for his tricherie, þe trewest on erþe:
Hit watz Ennias þe athel, and his highe kynde,
Þat siþen depreced prouinces, and patrounes bicome
Welneȝe of al þe wele in þe west iles.
Fro riche Romulus to Rome ricchis hym swyþe,
With gret bobbaunce þat burȝe he biges vpon fyrst,
And neuenes hit his aune nome, as hit now hat;
Tirius to Tuskan and teldes bigynnes,
Langaberde in Lumbardie lyftes vp homes,
And fer ouer þe French flod Felix Brutus
On mony bonkkes ful brode Bretayn he settez wyth wynne,
Where werre and wrake and wonder
Bi syþez hatz wont þerinne,
And oft boþe blysse and blunder
Ful skete hatz skyfted synne.[68]

The above passage can be translated thus:

'Since the siege and the assault of Troy ceased, when that city was destroyed and burnt all to ashes, and the traitor was tried for the treason he wrought, the nobleman Aeneas and his high kin plundered provinces and held in their power well nigh all the wealth of the western isles. Then Romulus, arriving swiftly in Rome, built that city and gave to it his name, which to this day it bears; Ticius turned to Tuscany and raised towns; while Langobard raised up dwellings in Lombardy; and far over the French flood Felix Brutus sailed and founded the kingdom of Britain with joy, where and waste and wonder have come to pass, and often both bliss and blunder have many times come and gone.'[69]

The Brutus myth was not the invention of the Gawain author. It is referred to in the *Historia Britonum* attributed to the ninth-century Welsh antiquary Nennius, and was popularised by Geoffrey of Monmouth (c.1100-1155), whose *Historia regum Britanniae* (*History of the Kings of Britain*)[70] devotes an entire chapter to Brutus' exploits. The Anglo-Norman poet Wace (c.1115-1180) also described the founding of Britain by Brutus of Troy in his *Roman de Brut* (c.1155),[71] which borrowed heavily from Geoffrey's work, and in turn inspired Laȝamon's thirteenth-century verse history of Britain, *Brut*.

According to the legend, Brutus led his followers to a promised island 'beyond the setting of the sun, past the realms of Gaul' to establish *altera troia* ('a second Troy'), and was told in a dream: 'A race of kings will be born there from your stock and the round circle of the whole earth will be subject to them.' All subsequent kings of England were held to be descendants of Brutus.

Daniel Birkholz argues that 'This invocation of prehistory establishes the imperial patrimony and destiny of Britain's kings' and is a means of legitimising and/or promoting Edward I's kingship – which implies that the original map would have been made with the King very much in mind. Edward I had attended the opening of Arthur's Tomb at Glastonbury in 1278, so he was very much aware of the power of what might be described as the Arthurian brand. The mention of Brutus can be interpreted as a further endorsement of the King's status, which was in any case likely to be in the ascendancy following his recent conquest of Wales. We know, moreover, that Edward regarded Brutus as key to his claim on his next military objective – Scotland.

The throne of Scotland became vacant in 1286 with the death of King Alexander III. Since all his children had predeceased him, his four-year-old grand-daughter Margaret – whose mother had married the King of Norway – was named as his successor. Edward hoped to secure a union between England and Scotland by marrying his son Edward of Caernarvon to Margaret, but though it was arranged for the Maid of Norway (as she became known) to make the journey from Scandinavia in 1290, she died in the Orkneys en route. There followed the dispute between thirteen rival claimants to the crown known as the Great Cause, in which Edward successfully supported John de Baliol, only to see the Scots rebel in 1295 and make a treaty with his enemy Philip IV of France.

Edward's successful invasion of Scotland in 1296, and his removal of the symbolic Stone of Scone to Westminster Abbey, brought him into conflict with Pope Boniface VII, who in 1299 issued a bull demanding that he end his northern wars since 'from ancient times the realm of Scotland belonged rightfully, and is still known to belong, to the Roman church'. On 7 May 1301 Edward sent a reply in which he outlined his own credentials as English overlord of Scotland.

His letter traced Edward's claim through Brutus' heirs – including King Arthur, who 'subjected to himself a rebellious Scotland'. Since that time, Edward claims, 'in succession all the Kings of Scotland have been subject to all the Kings of the Britons'. It is no wonder, then, that the Gough Map should seek to present Brutus's landing in Devon as a matter of historical and geographical fact.

The Victorian commentator on the Gough Map, W.B. Sanders, suggested that there might also be a reference to the Scottish succession in the shipwreck depicted in the north-eastern corner between the *Insula de Orkeney* and Norway. The ship is of a type built in the early fourteenth century[72] (though this is probably more useful for dating the map than dating the incident shown on it), and Parsons suggests that the rocks are possibly the Pentland Skerries, which are included on Mercator's map of Britain of 1564 with the warning 'Here be dangerous rockes called Petlant skerres'.

The wreck, Sanders hypothesised, could represent the fatal end of the final voyage undertaken by the Maid of Norway. However, among the few documents that exist there is some evidence of the Maid's arrival at Orkney and death there, there is no record of a shipwreck. William Rishanger, a contemporary writer, states that she was taken ill on the voyage and died at Orkney. On 8 September 1290 John Tyndale brought word to Edward I of the Maid's arrival in Orkney. In 1320 it was recorded in a letter dated 1 February by Bishop Audfinn in Bergen that the Maid 'died in Orkney attended by Bishop Narve, and in the presence of the best men who followed her from Norway as counselled and directed by her own father'.

Parsons suggests instead that the incident shown may derive from the *Orkneyinga Saga*'s account of the life of the Earl Rögnvald, Lord of Shetland, who was shipwrecked at Gulberwick, near what is now Lerwick, in about 1150 when crossing from Moray. This begs the question, however, of why his fate should be given prominence on a map devoted to the whole of Britain.

Another possibility is that the drawing has a symbolic function. Daniel Birkholz points out that the metaphor of 'the ship of state' had currency at the time, and that the distressed vessel could represent Scotland. The incomplete drawing next to it, which seems to show a figure leaning from a second boat, might then represent Edward I coming to the rescue of a country wrecked by the dispute over its next ruler. Birkholz finds further symbolism in the three large sea creatures shown to the south of the ships, suggesting that the apparent battle of a whale against a thrasher and a swordfish could represent England's struggle against Wales and Scotland.

Degrees of Accuracy

I N TERMS OF OVERALL ACCURACY, Scotland, Wales and Cornwall, on the map's peripheries, appear least like the outlines one would expect to see today. These areas, with the exception of Wales, are also devoid of the red route lines.[73] The shape of Scotland was seemingly not known to the cartographer, as it is drawn as a peninsula protruding northwards with indentations for mouths of rivers, which vary markedly in terms of accuracy, or indeed reality.

Scotland's rectilinear configuration (which lacks the north-eastern bearings of the east coast from Dundee to Peterhead and from Dornoch to Wick, and the north-facing coast from Fraserburgh to Nairn) gives the impression that the north to south extent of Britain is exaggerated. This is reinforced by the fact that the north to south extent of England errs slightly in the opposite direction.

ENGLAND AND WALES

In southern England the overall distances are relatively correct among themselves. The distance from Dover to Land's End corresponds to a scale of 1:1,000,000 and this is true also of the distances from London to Norwich, London to St David's and London to Caernarvon. The Thames Estuary and the Bristol Channel are in good relationship, as are Berwick-upon-Tweed and the Solway Firth. The main disfigurement of the southern portion of the map lies in the narrowness of the south-western peninsula and the outline given to Wales. The omission of Cardigan Bay and the exaggeration of the north-to-south extent of Wales are the principal errors, making it too large and also confusing the topography of the interior.

The general bearing of the west coast north-north-west from Liverpool to Solway Firth is good, but there is a major error in the omission of Morecambe Bay. A line drawn across this part of England from Preston to Hull also corresponds to the scale of 1:1,000,000. The general bearing north-north-west of the east coast from The Wash to Berwick is correct. The north Norfolk coast and the Thames estuary are very well delineated and Foulness, Sheppey, and Thanet are shown as islands in approximately their correct positions.

Most of the principal features of the south coast as a whole are indicated, though the bays are not sufficiently pronounced: Lyme Bay, for instance, is flattened out and Southampton Water is inconspicuous. The Isle of Wight appears for the first time in a recognisable form on a map. Portland and Selsey, whose 'bills' are important points for navigators, are represented as islands – as from the sea, Portland might easily appear to be. Other islands are shown, but these, in common with those off other coasts, are drawn on an exaggerated scale. A sandbank is shown in the mouth of the River Exe.

The overall accuracy of the proportions given to Great Britain cannot be dismissed as chance. General overall length and breadth figures had been estimated for Great Britain by classical authors:[74] Pliny had put it at 800 miles long and 300 miles broad. and this was quoted on the Corpus Christi College Cambridge copy of the Matthew Paris map held in the Parker Library. But for the Gough Map, it is almost certain that measurements of some kind were available from which the compiler was able to produce the correct distances quoted earlier. The only visible indication of the compiler's concern with distances other than those relating to routes appears on the island of Anglesey, where it is stated that the island is 24 miles in longitude and 18 in latitude.

Edward Lynam argued in his book *British maps and map-makers*[75] that most of England and Wales must have been surveyed to provide the detail for this map, and suggested some form of triangulation performed with the astrolabe. This, however, is very unlikely as there is no evidence for this type of operation in medieval times.[76] The study of astronomy was well advanced in England in the fourteenth century, and the work of the Merton astronomers at Oxford had acquired a world-wide reputation,[77] so it is quite possible for latitudes to have been computed from the stars and used to obtain the north-south accuracy of the map; but longitudes were another matter. It is true that they had been worked out for London, Hereford,[78] Oxford, Colchester and Berwick[79] by this time, and perhaps for other towns, but they were prepared principally for astronomical and astrological purposes.

Since triangulation and longitude must be ruled out, the compiler could only have based his measurements on those known for routes. From the itineraries of the day it would be possible to work out overall distances and to build up a fairly accurate picture of the proportions of the country and the location of the rivers and major towns.

As for the placing of the vignettes, this has obviously been done with much care. Sometimes, because of overcrowding, a town symbol has been placed on the wrong bank of a river, but on all the map except for northern Scotland the degree of accuracy calls for the greatest admiration, and several groups of towns are correctly placed in relation to each other at the scale of 1:1,000,000.

SCOTLAND

In contrast to England, Scotland is represented in a crude fashion: the coast and rivers, where outlined in ink, are far less distinct than those in England, and the detail in the northern part is confused. It is of interest, however, to consider what knowledge of the country the map records. The outline is narrow and tongue-shaped, stretching out due north from England and broken by inadequate representations of the great inlets. The most conspicuous of these is the wedge-shaped Firth of Forth, which, with the River Teith, forms the eastern section of a waterway running right across Scotland and isolating the north, except for a bridge west of Stirling. The western end of the waterway is just to the north of the Clyde and appears to incorporate Loch Lomond. This is one of the most persistent features of the early cartography of Scotland:[80] it occurs on the earliest 'land maps' of any importance, on the Hereford *Mappa Mundi* and on one of the Matthew Paris maps[81] – as well as portolan charts – though its precise location varies.

On the east coast, the Spey has Inverness at its mouth and is shown as flowing due east from the middle of the country. The Don and the Dee are confused, and so are the North and South Esk. Errors of this kind have naturally thrown out the topography of the interior, but on the whole some appreciation of the main features of southern Scotland is shown.

No attempt has been made to suggest the fretted and broken coasts of the west, and the main feature is the Clyde, correctly shown as a very broad river flowing from the south-east. The straightness of this coast northwards from Argyll, and the lack of names of definite landmarks, make it difficult to state where errors have been made and what they are. Some indication, however, has been given of the western islands. Part of Argyll including Kintyre is shown as islands, and to the west of these is the island of Bute with a castle and forest. To the south of this group is what is probably the Isle of Arran. The Hebrides are shown by several islands, one of which bears the words *Les Outisles*. The island immediately to the north is probably (from the few readable letters of its name) meant to be Iona, and if this is so then the island upon which *Les Outisles* is written is Mull. This position agrees with that given by George Lily on his map *Britanniae Insulae* of 1546.

The islands extend round the north to the *Mare acquilonare* (North Sea), where the largest island is named *Insula de Orkeney* and has a river and four towns (Kirkwall is the only one named). They are in approximately this position on the Matthew Paris map (*Cotton MS Claudius D. vi*), and since many portolan charts also show a large island in this position it would seem that this feature as well as the 'insularity' of northern Scotland originated with land maps.

Owing to the narrow shape of Scotland, Loch Tay is shown well east of Dunkeld and Dull (Perthshire). Elgin and Darnaway are placed far inland, and Wick becomes the most northerly town in Scotland.

GEORECTIFICATION

Reference has already been made in the preface to the recent work undertaken by DigiData Technologies, whereby the Gough Map has been georectified using British national grid co-ordinates to produce a striking analysis of the map's accuracy. This has made it possible to hypothesize, seven centuries after its creation, where the map could have been made, based on the assumption that its compiler must have had – like most people – a better knowledge of the country close to where he was based than of more distant parts of it. (See the following chapter, however, for an alternative view.)

The usual procedure in historic rectification is to take a map from a previous era and match it to a contemporary map of the same area, by changing its projection and/or scale.[82] The matching depends on finding points known as Ground Control Points (GCPs) which appear on both. GCPs are graded for dependability according to how little or how much they are likely to have changed in the intervening period: 'higher order' control points are features such as churches which are known not to have altered their shape or position; 'lower order' control points are features such as rivers which are more than likely to have done so. The problem with the Gough Map is that parts of Britain (particularly, as we have seen, in Scotland and Wales) are presented so inaccurately that a direct comparison with a modern map is exceedingly difficult.

On the other hand, the Gough Map does have, in its symbols for settlements, a wealth of GCPs which can be matched with modern cities, towns and villages. (One of the hopes in undertaking the georectification project was that some of the places whose names were missing or indecipherable could be identified in the process, though this work has yet to be done.) Modern technology made it possible to match 408 of these, using computers to work out the minimum stretching or distortion of the Gough Map required to bring the corresponding points together. The fact that a facsimile of the map had been published by the Ordnance Survey (first in 1871 and again 1935),[83] giving clear translations of the textual content, helped this process considerably.

To gauge the amount of displacement each point has to undergo relative to its neighbouring points, the computers calculated a value called the Root Mean Square (RMS). The average of the distances between each pair of control points is known as the Root Mean Square Error (RMSE): the lower this is, the greater the similarity of geometry between the two maps.

With the Gough Map, some of the RMSES were enormous – especially those for Scotland (though many of the main towns and cities in the Lowlands had unexpectedly low ones). By removing Scotland from the equation, however, it was possible to arrive at some fascinating discoveries. The next poorest fits were those of the north of England, the Welsh coast and the tip of Cornwall; more surprisingly, some high levels of inaccuracy were detected at certain points along the Channel coast and Essex coast. The best fits, on the other hand, were to be found in a band between Devon and Norfolk (Exeter is very well placed), and most particularly in a broad sweep between Oxford and Cambridge, where the top 5 per cent of matching points lay. If correct, this would suggest that the map housed in the Bodleian Library may be preserved a relatively short distance from where it was created.

DVI

Padſtou

Tintogd

BI

Launſton

Hertlond

A

xanton

Bidford

DE

khornel

chilmeil

Baſtable

Molton

VONI

A

ONIA

SOMER

SE

TV

S

ord

charde

Ilcheſter

ſehirborn

ſhaftiſbury

WILCE

RI

A

BRISTO

BATHO

NI

A

Barklei

malinſburi

SARIS BVRIA

ordingbrige

Almiſburi

chipnam

Holms

Milford

S. DAVID

Kilgaren

cardigan

Aberwy

PENB

RVCH

Arſord

ſtretflor

NORTH

Tinbi

Kidwelle

WAL

Towe

caſt.melip

werei

crykky

SOVTH

caermardin

caſt.nouũ

Moith. f

ſtuamſei

WAL

ſtrodmore

caernar

Neth

LI

Marget

Landuri

A

veius. f

Landuri

S. ASAPH

Landaffa

Abergeny

SABRINA. F

Pole

con

wethrin

A

oſweſtir

Rutuin

Neuport

Hay

Logus. f

wigmore

SALO

flint

chepſto

Monmouth

PI

A

ROS

Ludlon

Lirpol

HERE

CESTRI

Dene foreſta

FOR

DI

A

A

Liſil

Halton

Brignorih

caſtr. nouũ

GLOCES

TRI

VIGOR

STAFOR

warington

Teukiſbiri

A

NIA

DI

A

marlboro

wmehcomb

Hailes

Lichfeld

Aſchborn

BERCHE

deruent. f

Andouer

Hungerford

RI

ſtratfort

WARVICVM

DER

A

burton

BI

ſouthwel

TONIA

Nubery

OXONIVM

couentria

A

ſhe

TONA

Baſingſtok

Re

ding

Abington

vodſlok

LECESTRIA

NOTINGA

ſchirwod

Alton

Dorcheſter

MIA

odiham

Henlei

NORTHAM

dancaſter

STRIA

winde

ſora

maidenhed

TO

NA

ſtanford

Newark

SVS

chedingfeld

Gilſord

BOKINGAMIA

BEDFOR

Ancaſter

SEX

DI

A

IA

Kingſton

colbrok

HERTFOR

ſtelton

LINCOLNIA

SVRRE

LONDI

DIA

Baldoc

donſtable

NVM

Peterborow

HVNTIGTO

Boſton

NA

Luth

Grimſby

The Map's Legacy

O N COMPLETION, the Gough Map does not appear to have needed updating for around 250 years. There were relatively few maps produced in Britain until mapmaking on a national scale was revolutionised in the 1570s by Christopher Saxton, whose Crown-sponsored atlas of the counties of England and Wales was richly detailed in terms of boundaries, settlements, rivers, uplands, forests, parks, though interestingly not in terms of roads.

The Gough Map clearly became well-known internationally, as its outline remained in use by cartographers overseas for almost two centuries. Two continental maps from the 1540s very clearly rely on Gough for their inspiration. These are the map of England in Sebastian Münster's edition of Ptolemy's *Geographia* produced in Basle in Switzerland in 1540,[84] and the engraved map of the British Isles of 1546 generally attributed to George Lily.

Münster's woodcut map is considerably smaller than the Gough Map, measuring 25 by 34 cm (9¹/⁴ by 13¹/² inches), but comparing it with a reduced version of the latter reveals definite similarities. East is at the top, the names read from north to south, and the outline and rivers are much alike. Cardigan Bay fails to appear; there is agreement on small details such as the Essex coastline, the rivers around Axholme and Ely, the position of Anglesey and Priestholm, the islands in the Bristol Channel, and the delineation of Loch Ryan in Scotland (though much of the rest of Scotland is excluded). Manhood in Sussex (the coastal peninsula area between Chichester and Selsey) – named Manwich by Münster, and Manwod on the Gough Map – is shown as an island, and the mistake of presenting Dartmoor as a lake is repeated.

George Lily's copperplate map *Britanniae Insulae*,[85] produced in Rome six years later, is very much akin to the Gough Map and Münster's in most of the details mentioned above. It does, however, have a greater geographical extent, taking in all of Ireland and far more of northern France; and it places west rather than east at the top of the map. Again, Cardigan Bay is not present, but Lily's mapping of Scotland is altogether more accurate.

FIGURE 10 (detail left and overleaf)
George Lily's *Britanniae Insulae*,
British Library. Maps K. Top. 5 (1).

FIGURE 11 (pp. 54-55)
Sebastian Münster's *Anglia II
Nova Tabula* (1540),
British Library. Maps C. 1. c. 2.

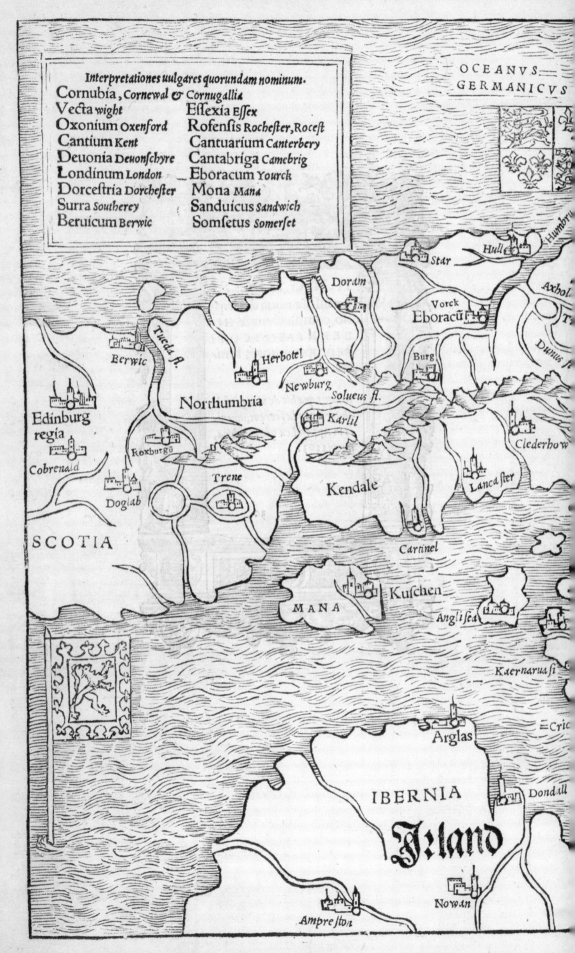

Interpretationes uulgares quorundam nominum.

Cornubia, Cornewal & Cornugallia
Vecta wight
Oxonium Oxenford
Cantium Kent
Deuonia Deuonschyre
Londinum London
Dorcestria Dorchester
Surra Southerey
Beruicum Berwic

Essexia Essex
Rosensis Rochester, Rocest
Cantuarium Canterbery
Cantabriga Camebrig
Eboracum Yourck
Mona Mana
Sanduicus sandwich
Somsetus Somset

OCEANVS
GERMANICVS

Hull
Humbrum
Star
Axhol.
Doram
Vorck
Eboracū
Dunus fl.
Berwic
Tueda fl.
Herbotel
Burg
Newburg
Solueus fl.
Northumbria
Karlil
Clederhow
Edinburg regia
Roxburgū
Cobrenald
Trene
Kendale
Lancaster
Doglab
SCOTIA
Cartinel
MANA
Kuschen
Anglisea
Kaernarua fl.
Cric
Arglas
IBERNIA
Dondall
Irland
Nowan
Ampreston

Cales · Bolonge S.Ios · Artois

PICARDIA

Tenet · Sant Vic · Douer · Lyt · Diepñ

Caux

Nortfol · Soutfolck · Canterby · Hafting

Essex · Cantiũ Rofeñ

Chemiford · Tameñs fl. · Soutbrey

Cantabriga · Lewig · Mare Anglicũ

Ely · Herteford · London · Soutfex

Peterburg · Bedfort · S.Alban · Silford

ford · Arondel · Manwid

Reding · Niport · Vuight · NOR MAN DIA

Couentre · warwick · Oxonium · Casquet

Lichefild · Hamtõ

Stasford worceter · Tamefis · Grenze · Mons fancti Michaelis

Gloceter · Salisberi Dorcestria

Hereford · Sabrina fl. · Schirborn

Vuallia · Velus fl. · Briftow

Holmis · Brigwater

Somfet · Exceter

Deuonia · Molts · CORNVBIA

Keltertyn · Leskerd

Caerdigan · Limiday · Corneual

Arford · Calday · S.Colomb · Falmoüth

BRITANNIA

Kamfey · S.Yos

Suirus fl. · Vatford · S.Penrin

This map is larger than Münster's at 53.5 by 74.5 cm (21 by 29¹/⁴ inches), but is still much smaller than the Gough Map. Both Lily and Münster also show the main ranges of hills and mountains, some of which are lacking on the Gough Map.

A third map which probably owed something to the southern part of the Gough Map is the one published by Mercator in 1564.[86] Material was sent out to him from England by an unidentified correspondent, and his map was produced at approximately the same scale. Obviously later material was to hand for the coastline and rivers, but for information on the towns the Gough Map would have been very valuable, and most of those it includes also appear on the Mercator map.

However, closer to the Gough Map than any other seems to be the relatively recently 'discovered' map found on the verso of folios in a sixteenth-century manuscript at Yale University in 1962.[87] This is a map primarily of England and Wales, inserted into a book which also includes a table of routes and distances on the verso. The map itself measures a modest 18 by 26 cm (8 by 10¹/⁴ inches) and includes some 250 locations. It was sketched by the book's owner, an Essex-based merchant named Thomas Butler, some time between 1547 and 1554, and the resultant map is most definitely not constructed in the contemporary cartographic style. The majority of towns are marked by a red circle; York, Canterbury and six other towns by a red spire/triangle; and London by a triangle flanked by two circles. There are nine castles with moats; county towns are identified; there are boxed country and region names; and rivers are marked by faint lines.

FIGURE 12
Butler's *Mape off Ynglonnd*, Beinecke Rare Book and Manuscript Library, Yale University. Beibecke MS. 558

East is at the top of the map, Cardigan Bay is missing, and Scotland shows signs of assuming a similar shape, despite being cut off just north of the central lowland valley. This map is considerably more comprehensive than those of Münster or Lily, and therefore must be a copy of the Gough Map, though the rivers are less prominent, no distances are included, and more detail is shown in Ireland.

Although the distances on the Gough Map are repeated in the road books of the sixteenth century, it seems (as mentioned earlier) that routes with mileages were not included on a map of Britain again until Thomas Jenner's *The kingdome of England & principality of Wales exactly described* … of 1671.

It says much for the Gough Map's compiler that many of its distance figures appear as computed mileages in Ogilby's *Britannia* of 1675 more than three centuries later.[88]

THE PRESENT AND FUTURE

The new opportunities for exploring the Gough Map have already been alluded to in the Preface. As Catherine Delano-Smith wrote in support of the proposal to scan the map for the Oxford Digital Library:

'The (apparent) uniqueness of the Gough Map poses a problem with wide-ranging implications in all sorts of directions (why it was made, where the material came from, what function it served, who paid for it, where it was executed – it is a remarkably skilled artefact for what was probably a wholly one-off project thought up by a strikingly idiosyncratic ... individual...).

'If answers to such questions are ever to be ventured, and light on the context of the map ever to be shed, it is essential to have ready access to as technically clear a reproduction as possible'.[89]

Now that access has been made possible, thanks to the work of DigiData Technologies, the focus for future research is the *Mapping the Realm* project undertaken by scholars from Queen's University Belfast in collaboration with the Bodleian Library.[90] This has involved the creation of a digital, GIS-based version of the map known as 'the digital Gough', enhancing the original to help identify its features and then linking these to a database. The latter has been constructed around Parsons' gazetteer of the map (reproduced in the Appendix); in addition, national grid references are given for all the places shown on the map.

The first use the digital Gough has been put to, by Keith Lilley and Chris Lloyd of Queen's University, is to analyse the map's accuracy by examining the positioning of the settlements on it.[91] Although this continuing exercise has some similarities to the georectification discussed in the last chapter, the methodology – and the findings made so far – are quite different. The procedure is to identify the more and less accurate parts of the map not by altering its size and shape, but by comparing the locations of places shown on it in 'map space' with the true positions given by their national grid co-ordinates.

The conclusion the initial results point to is that there is no single area of England, Scotland or Wales which is depicted with much greater accuracy than the rest (although as a general rule there is more accuracy south of a line between the Severn and the Humber than north of it). Instead, there are – right across the map – pockets of places which are located with outstanding precision. These are found as far apart as northern Scotland and the belt of country between Dorset and the Thames Estuary, north Cornwall and north-east England. Intriguingly, these findings suggest that the route network is not vital to the accuracy of the map, since some of the best-presented areas are beyond its reach.

Conversely, there are pockets of outstanding *in*accuracy in certain places, such as The Weald, the Hampshire Downs and the Chilterns. These tended to be sparsely populated areas – either because they were heavily forested or consisted of high ground – which implies a dependency on knowledge gathered from local inhabitants. Lloyd and Lilley believe that the map may indeed have been drawn up in conjunction with a survey conducted by the Exchequer, and may have had many contributors rather than a single creator.

Following on from this, a further project is envisaged over the next five years or so which will involve detailed analysis by specialists in a variety of fields, from art history to palaeography. It is unlikely to solve all the riddles wrapped in the mystery of the Gough Map – but there is every reason to hope that it will shed considerable further light on how medieval Britons perceived the country they inhabited.

Appendix:
Contents of the Map
by E.J.S. Parsons (1958)

T he place names, or the readable parts of them, together with their modern form, are arranged according to pre-1974 county. River names are listed separately in coastal groups. Three dots forming part of a name indicate that a letter or letters exist that are indecipherable. All abbreviations have been extended. The routes have been classified and the towns and distances listed. In this latter list, the modern form of the town name has been used.

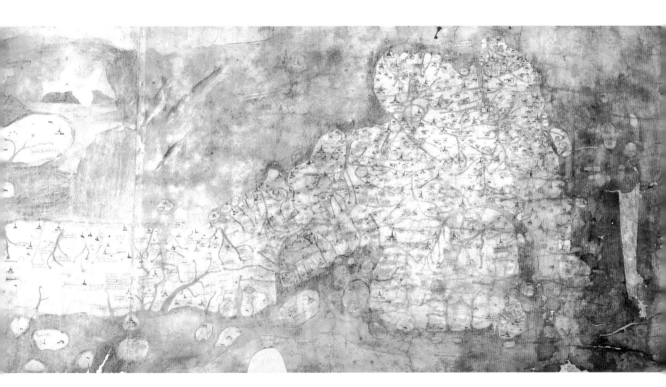

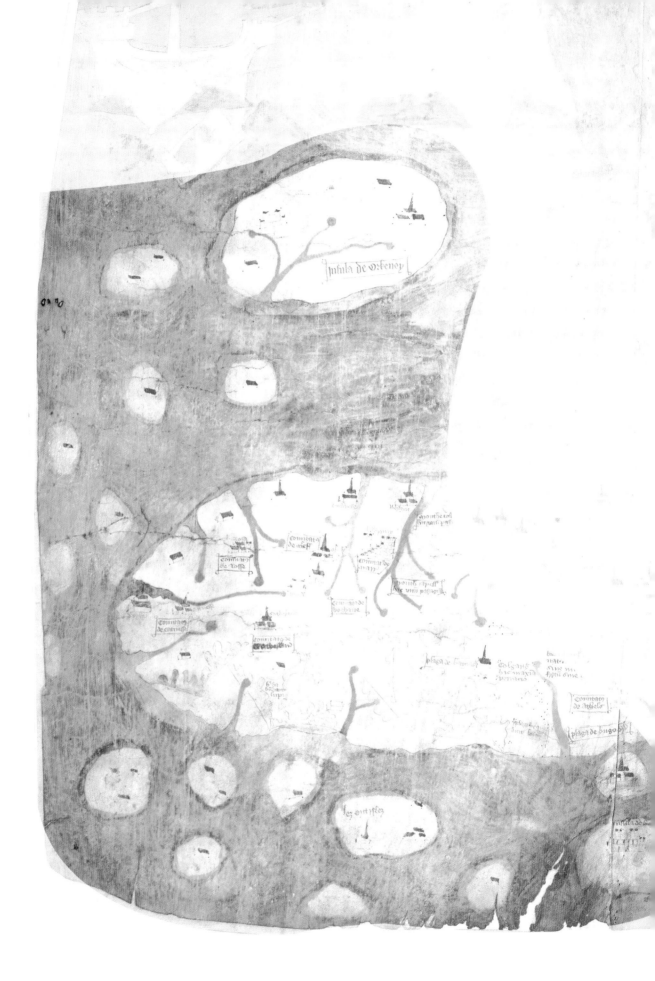

Insula de Orkenoy

comitatus de mieff

comitatus de Rossa

comitatus de entress

comitatus de Catheland

plaga de Lupo

les ort isles

comitatus de Affelo

plaga de hugo

Insula de

ABERDEENSHIRE

aberdene ABERDEEN, *kildromy* KILDRUMMY.

Within cartouches is written *Comitatus de marr* EARLDOM OF MARR and *Comitatus de boghane* EARLDOM OF BUCHAN. Also within a cartouche is written *Month capell hic unum passagium*. This is a pass through the Grampians which runs from Glen Clova to Glen Muick. West of Aberdeen is a symbol of which I do not know the meaning.

CAITHNESS

Catnesse CASTLE SINCLAIR ? *Wyke* WICK.

There is no town named Caithness today. Yet it appeared on Mercator's British Isles of 1564, on Speed's map of 1610, and on Camden's *Britannia* for 1637, as north or north-east of Wick. Speed narrows the area for *Catnesse* to between Girnego Castle and Wick. In all probability it refers to Castle Sinclair, chief stronghold of the earls of Caithness. Westwards from *Catnesse* across a river a town is shown with an indecipherable name, probably THURSO. Within a cartouche is written *Comitatus de Catnesse* EARLDOM OF CAITHNESS.

INVERNESS-SHIRE

...nagh BADENOCH, *Envernesse* INVERNESS.

Badenoch is shown on Speed's map of Scotland of 1610 and on Mercator's British Isles of 1564. It may refer, as Gough suggests, to Ruthven or Kingussie, but I think it refers to the castle of the Comyns at Loch am Eilein. Within a cartouche is written *plaga de barnagh* which Gough interprets rightly as the Badenoch region. To the south of Badenoch is written *Colgarth hic maxima venacio,* and to the west is a drawing of a deer. Gough places this between Badenoch and Atholl as the district now known as Gaick Forest which has been noted for its red deer for centuries, and I would agree.

MORAYSHIRE

terneway DARNAWAY, *Elgy* ELGIN, *murref'*.

There is no such town as Moray today but the *murref'* might well have referred either to the cathedral church of Moray at Elgin – the 'lantern of the north' – or to the episcopal palace at Spynie. Within a cartouche is written *Comitatus de murref'* EARLDOM OF MURRAY.

FIGURE 13

Aberdeenshire, Caithness, Inverness-shire, Morayshire, Orkney, Ross and Cromarty, Sutherland, and the Western Isles.

ORKNEY ISLANDS

These are shown off the north-east coast and the largest is labelled *Insula de Orkeney*. On this island are four towns, all with indecipherable names except the most southerly which is named *Kirkwall*. All the town names on the other islands are indecipherable.

ROSS AND CROMARTY

rosse DINGWALL.

The town of Dingwall sheltered under the neighbouring castle of the earls of Ross. On the coast north of Inverness is a town, probably FORTROSE, but the name is indecipherable. East of Dingwall is another town with an indecipherable name, possibly TAIN. Within a cartouche is written *Comitatus de Rosse* EARLDOM OF ROSS.

SUTHERLAND

sutherland DUNROBIN ?

There is no town named Sutherland today. The compiler of the Gough Map probably meant Dunrobin which was the seat of the Duke of Sutherland. North of Ross is a town with an indecipherable name which might be DORNOCH, and west of Sutherland is another which I cannot identify. Close to this town is a drawing of a wolf and written below it is *hic habundant lupi*. Within a cartouche is written *Comitatus de Sutherland* EARLDOM OF SUTHERLAND.

WESTERN ISLES

These are shown off the west coast. On the largest is written *Les Outisles*. On the island to the north of this one I can make out the letters *ona*, which would of course be IONA. This would make its southern neighbour Mull and would be similar to the arrangement on the Lily map of 1546.
All the town names on the other islands are indecipherable.

ANGUS

abrebrothok ARBROATH, *drighyn* BRECHIN, *dundee* DUNDEE, *Forfar* FORFAR, *Glammyes* GLAMIS, *mulrosse* MONTROSE.

Underneath *abrebrothok* is written *fundatur in honore sancti Thome Cant.* This refers to the abbey founded in 1178 by William, King of Scotland. It is dedicated to St Thomas of Canterbury.

ARGYLLSHIRE

Part of Argyll and Kintyre are shown as islands. On the northern island is portrayed a group of buildings named *argayell* which may refer to INVERARAY and on the southern island three towns are indicated, only one with a decipherable name *killecar…* KILKERRAN. On the mainland within a cartouche is written *Plaga que dicit. Loren* DISTRICT OF LORNE.

BUTESHIRE

The ISLE OF BUTE is labelled *Insula de bote* and on it is placed a town with an indecipherable name but which must be ROTHESAY. South of the island representing Kintyre is another island which could be the ISLE OF ARRAN. It has three towns indicated but the names of two are indecipherable; the third, the most northerly, could be ARRAN.

DUNBARTONSHIRE

Cumbrenald CUMBERNAULD, *dunbretayne* DUMBARTON.

Within a cartouche is written *Comitatus de levenay* EARLDOM OF LENNOX.

FIFESHIRE AND KINROSS-SHIRE

culross CULROSS, *dunferml…* DUNFERMLINE, *kyngor…*KINGHORN, *Sancti Andree* ST ANDREWS.
Loch Leven castle is shown but the name is indecipherable. Within a cartouche is written *Comitatus de Fyf* EARLDOM OF FIFE and just south of Loch Leven is the drawing of a hill labelled *lomond mons* LOMOND HILLS.

KINCARDINESHIRE

Colly COWIE, *enderburi* INVERBERVIE.

North of *Colly* within a cartouche is written *Monthe colli hic unum passagium.* This is shown as passing through a range of mountains (the Grampians) which cross the country from west to east. Gough suggests that this is the Cairn o'Mounth road but the modern view is that the Cowie Monthe is intended.

PERTHSHIRE

Coupar' COUPAR ANGUS, *dull* DULL, *dunblane* DUNBLANE, *Dunkeldyn* DUNKELD, *Sa. Joh.* PERTH, *Stone* SCONE.

West of Perth is a town with an indecipherable name – probably INCHAFFRAY. At the junction of the Forth and Teith is written within a cartouche *hic passagium de drippes.* This refers to the ford at Drip which is mentioned in Hardyng's *Chronicle.* To the west is a bridge labelled *Pons Aghmore.* This is not Achmore, as supposed by Sanders, but probably refers to a bridge at Callander which was overlooked by the Uaighmor and close to the Roman fort at Bochastle. Within cartouches are also written *Comitatus de Strathere* EARLDOM OF STRATHEARN, *Comitatus de Athels* EARLDOM OF ATHOLL, *Plaga de bugodre* DISTRICT OF BALQUHIDDER, and *Comitatus de Menteth* EARLDOM OF MENTEITH. LOCH TAY is drawn in and named and by it is written '*in isto lacu tria mirabilia insula natans pisces sine intestinis fretum sine vento*'. Gough comments that Scottish authors usually describe Loch Lomond in this manner. Just north of the Firth of Tay is written *Cas of Goure* CARSE OF GOWRIE. To the west of Loch Tay is a small symbol which I cannot identify.

STIRLINGSHIRE

skanskennett CAMBUSKENNETH, *stevelyn* STIRLING.

FIGURE 14
Angus, Argyllshire, Buteshire, Dunbartonshire, Fifeshire and Kinross-shire, Kincardineshire, Perthshire, and Stirlingshire.

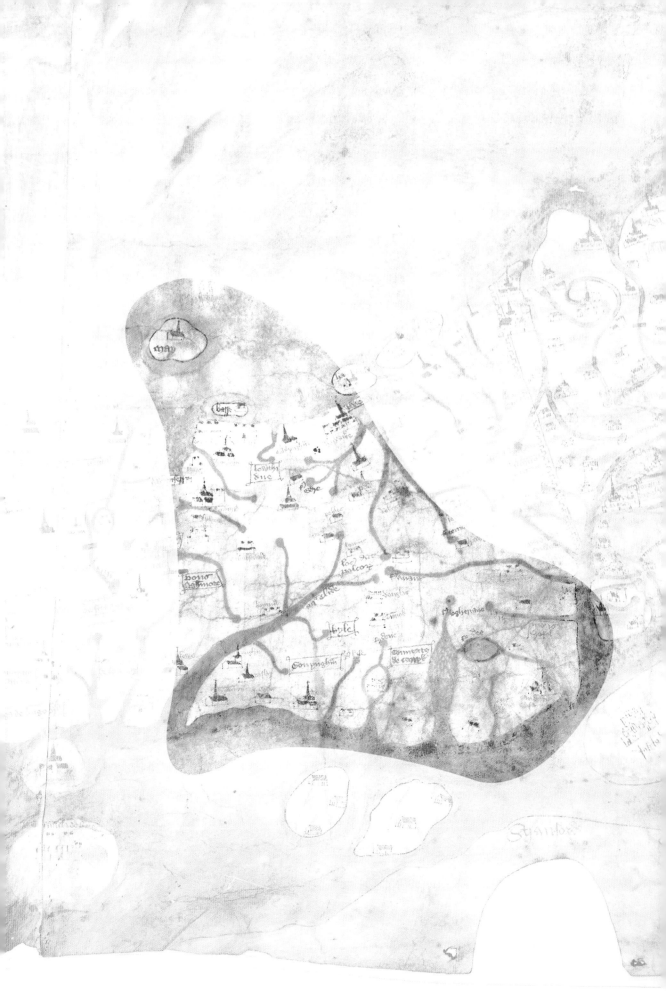

AYRSHIRE

are AYR, *Cunnok* CUMNOCK, *irwyn* IRVINE, *kynwenyn* KILWINNING, *lochdone* LOCH DOON CASTLE. South of Ayr across *fl. Kile* is a town with the name obliterated. South-west of Loch Doon is another town with an indecipherable name which could be CROSSRAGUEL. There are three province names given within cartouches; they are *Comitatus de Carryk* CARRICK, *kyle* KYLE, and *Conyngham* CUNNINGHAM.

BERWICKSHIRE

Coldyngham COLDINGHAM, *lowdere* LAUDER.

DUMFRIESSHIRE

Anan ANNAN, *carlaveroc* CAERLAVEROCK, *dromfres* DUMFRIES, *loghmaben* LOCHMABEN. East of Annan and across the Esk is written *Vada de Sulway* SOLWAY FIRTH.

EAST LOTHIAN

dunbarr' DUNBAR, *hadyngton* HADDINGTON, *hales* HAILES, *dentalonne* TANTALLON. Within a cartouche is written *lowthiane*. Off the coast is an island with a town indicated with the word *basse* written on it, i.e. BASS ROCK. Beyond Bass Rock is another island labelled *may*. Upon this island a town is indicated with indecipherable writing underneath.

KIRKCUDBRIGHTSHIRE

There are no towns shown in Kirkcudbrightshire, but a hill has been drawn in on the coast and labelled *mons Crofel* MOUNT CRIFFELL.

LANARKSHIRE

bygar BIGGAR, *boyuill* BOTHWELL, *Croweford* CRAWFORD, *douglas* DOUGLAS, *Glaskowe* GLASGOW, *lanarc* LANARK, *Ruglyn* RUTHERGLEN. West of Lanark is written *locus dictus polcorum*. Gough thought this referred to Bonieton (Bonnington). In the introduction to the *National manuscripts of Scotland* it is suggested that Corra linn is meant since 'pol' or 'pool' was a word frequently used in that district. I think both are right and that the phrase is a purely descriptive one. The name Lanark (from *Llanerch* 'a forest glade') sets the picture and the area includes the three celebrated Falls of Clyde, Bonnington, Corra, and Stonebyres Linns.

MIDLOTHIAN

Edenburgh EDINBURGH. Within a cartouche across the Forth is written *Whenfe*. This may well refer to the Queensferry which is recorded c.1295 as Queneferie, or it could have some connexion with Wemyss which before 1300 is recorded as Whense. It might refer to the river Forth, being written in the same manner as Twede, but *fl. forth* can be read at the source shown near Bothwell. South of Edinburgh and north of Peebles is a town with the name obliterated. This I think should be NEWBATTLE.

PEEBLESSHIRE

pebles PEEBLES.

RENFREWSHIRE

Paslay PAISLEY.

ROXBURGHSHIRE

hawyke HAWICK, *ermitage* HERMITAGE, *jedworth* JEDBURGH, *kelse* KELSO, *meltros* MELROSE, *Rokesburgh* ROXBURGH.

WEST LOTHIAN

lithcowe LINLITHGOW. North-east of Edinburgh is a town on the Firth of Forth with an indecipherable name; it is probably QUEENSFERRY.

WIGTOWNSHIRE

...well CORSEWALL, *Candida casa* WHITHORN, *wigton* WIGTOWN. North of Wigtown in a lake is a vignette with an indecipherable name which might be SOULSEAT.

FIGURE 15
Ayrshire, Berwickshire, Dumfriesshire, East Lothian, Kirkcudbrightshire, Lanarkshire, Midlothian, Peeblesshire, Renfrewshire, Roxburghshire, West Lothian, and Wigtownshire.

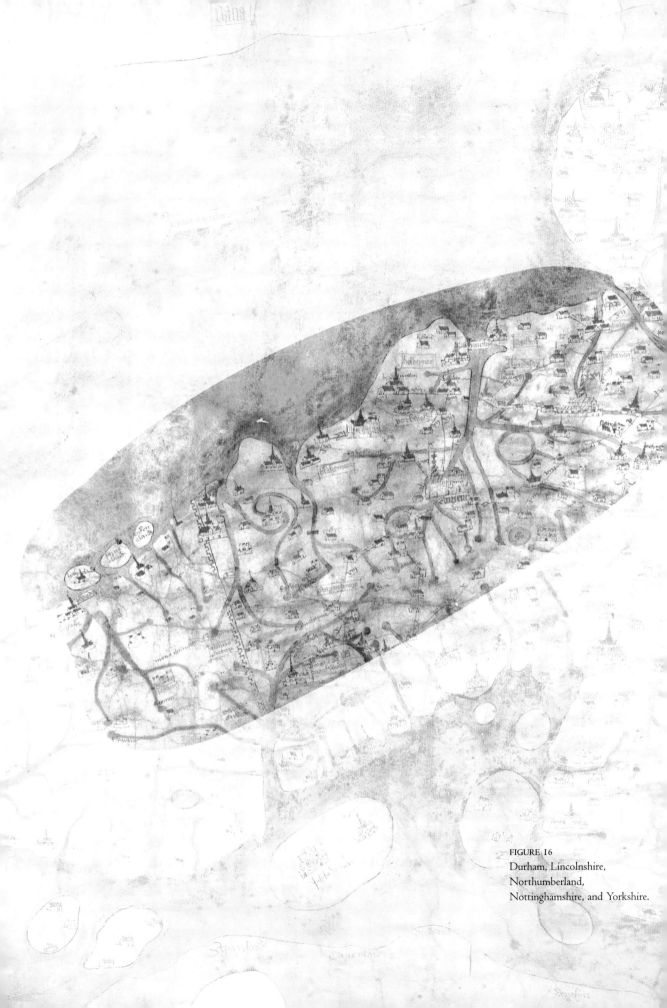

FIGURE 16
Durham, Lincolnshire,
Northumberland,
Nottinghamshire, and Yorkshire.

DURHAM

Castrum barnard BARNARD CASTLE, *aukeland* BISHOP AUCKLAND, *chestre* CHESTER LE STREET, *derlyngton* DARLINGTON, *dunelm* DURHAM, *esyngton* EASINGTON, *herthepoll* HARTLEPOOL, *persbrig* PIERCEBRIDGE, *sta...drop* STAINDROP, *stanhope* STANHOPE, *Wermouth* WEARMOUTH.

Piercebridge is wrongly sited on the south bank of the Tees. A bridge is shown over the river at this point.

LINCOLNSHIRE

ancastre ANCASTER, *bardne* BARDNEY, *barton* BARTON, *bilesfeld* BITCHFIELD, *bolingbrok* BOLINGBROKE, *Boston* BOSTON, *brune* BOURNE, *glanfordbrig* BRIGG, *burton-stather* BURTON-ON-STATHER, *cast...* CAISTOR, *Croweland* CROWLAND, *fosdyke* FOSDYKE, *grantham* GRANTHAM, *gremby* GRIMSBY, *horncastell* HORNCASTLE, *kirkton* KIRTON, *lincoln* LINCOLN, *louth* LOUTH, *pinchebek* PINCHBECK, *flete* SALTFLEET, *sleford* SLEAFORD, *Somerton* SOMERTON CASTLE, *spaldynge* SPALDING, *spitall* SPITAL-IN-THE-STREET, *Stamford* STAMFORD, *Stowe* STOW, *torkesey* TORKSEY, *Waynflet* WAINFLEET, *Wragby* WRAGBY.

O.S. 1935 read *bilesfeld* as Bilgfeld and *burton-stather* as Burtonleather. The island of Axholme is named *axiholm*. Within cartouches are given the district names of *holand* HOLLAND, *kesteven* KESTEVEN, *Ageland* AVELAND, *lyndesey* LINDSEY.

NORTHUMBERLAND

alnewik ALNWICK, *bamburgh* BAMBURGH, *Berwike* BERWICK, *bolton* BOLTON, *corbryg* CORBRIDGE, *felton* FELTON, *h...ston* HAGGERSTON, *hautwisel* HALTWHISTLE, *hbotell* HARBOTTLE, *haidon* HAYDON BRIDGE, *hexham* HEXHAM, *langley* LANGLEY, *morpeth* MORPETH, *Newebiggyn* NEWBIGGIN, *newbrough* NEWBROUGH, *novum castrum* NEWCASTLE-UPON-TYNE, *norham* NORHAM, *prodhowe* PRUDHOE, *rothbury* ROTHBURY, *thirlewall* THIRLWALL CASTLE, *tynmouth* TYNEMOUTH, *werk* WARK, *warkworth* WARKWORTH, *Wollere* WOOLER.

O.S. 1935 misread *thirlewall* as Reswall. The symbol for Morpeth has almost disappeared and was omitted on the 1935 reproduction. Across the county from the east coast at Tynemouth to the western border and beyond to the west coast is drawn one straight and one crenellated line labelled

murus pictorum HADRIAN'S WALL. To the north of this wall is the drawing of a mountain underneath which is written *mons chivioth* CHEVIOT HILLS. Off the coast are three islands. The most northerly has a town symbol and is named *haly eland* HOLY ISLAND; the other two have no symbols and are named *farne eland* FARNE ISLAND, and *Cokett eland* COQUET ISLAND.

NOTTINGHAMSHIRE

blith BLYTH, *maunsfeld* MANSFIELD, *mattersey* MATTERSEY, *Newerk* NEWARK, *Notyngham* NOTTINGHAM, *suthwell* SOUTHWELL, *tuxford* TUXFORD.

O.S. 1935 has Coxton for Tuxford, but Tuxford can be read under ultra-violet light. Two trees near Mansfield form a symbol for Sherwood Forest. The letters *s* and *w* of the name can just be seen.

YORKSHIRE

bawtri BAWTRY, *bentham* BENTHAM, *beverley* BEVERLEY, *burghbrig* BOROUGHBRIDGE, *bowes* BOWES, *bradford* BRADFORD, *brydlington* BRIDLINGTON, *bolton* CASTLE BOLTON, *Croft brig* CROFT, *doncastre* DONCASTER, *gyllyng* GILLING, *gesbogh* GUISBOROUGH, *morehouse* HAWES (formerly Horsehouse), *hedon* HEDON, *helme* HELMSLEY, *helperby* HELPERBY, *hesell* HESSLE, *hornsee* HORNSEA, *hawden* HOWDEN, *hull* HULL, *knaresburgh* KNARESBOROUGH, *langton* LANGTON, *ledes* LEEDS, *lyming* LEEMING, *malton* MALTON, *Wighton* MARKET WEIGHTON, *Allert...* NORTHALLERTON, *patryngton* PATRINGTON, *pickeringe* PICKERING, *poklington* POCKLINGTON, *pontfret* PONTEFRACT, *richemond* RICHMOND, *repon* RIPON, *...ch* ROCHE ABBEY, *roerham* ROTHERHAM, *scarbough* SCARBOROUGH, *semere* SEAMER, *sebergh* SEDBERGH, *Setell* SETTLE, *sheffeld* SHEFFIELD, *skipton* SKIPTON, *tadcastre* TADCASTER, *thresk* THIRSK, *tikhull* TICKHILL, *Wakefeld* WAKEFIELD, *Watre* WARTER, *Watton* WATTON, *Wederbie* WETHERBY, *Whitbi* WHITBY, *yarm* YARM, *Eboriens'* YORK.

O.S. 1935 misread *helperby* as Helm.... Leeds is placed on the wrong bank of the Aire. A bridge is shown over the Ure at Boroughbridge. Within cartouches are the following district names: *holdernes* HOLDERNESS, *yorkwold* THE WOLDS, *Blakemore* LOW AND HIGH BLAKEY MOOR, *Staynesmore* STAINMORE. These appear as district names on Saxton's map of 1577.

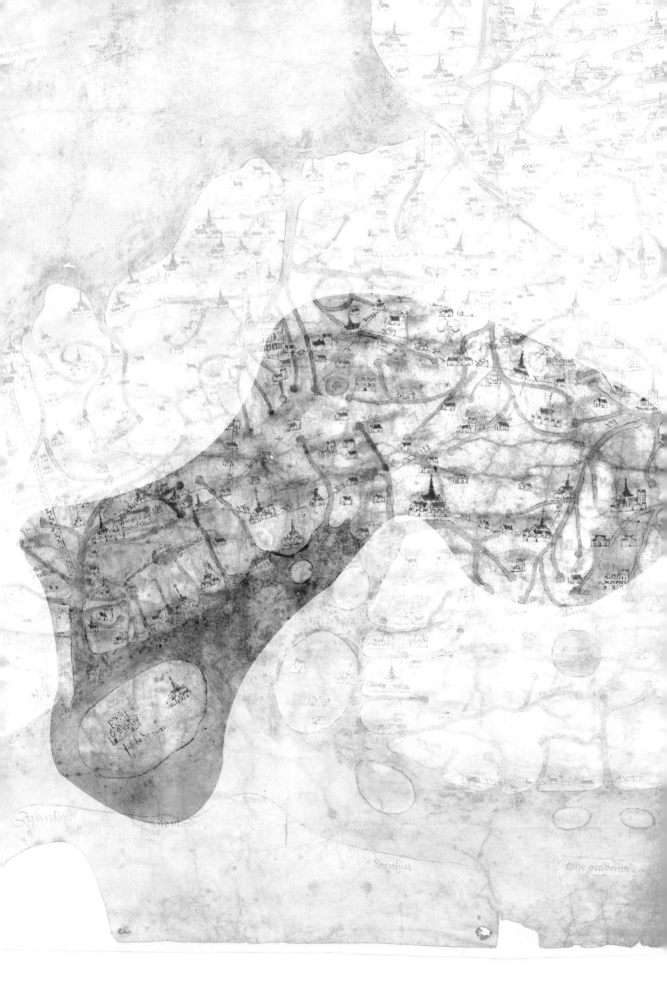

CHESHIRE

chestre CHESTER, *maxfeld* MACCLESFIELD, *wych* NANTWICH, *northw...* NORTHWICH

maxfeld was read as Mayfeld by O.S. 1935. *wych* was read as Worthin by Sanders.

CUMBERLAND

aldeston in Mora ALSTON, *bownes* BOWNESS, *bramton* BRAMPTON, *burgh juxta sablones* BURGH BY SANDS, *karlil* CARLISLE, *cokermouth* COCKERMOUTH, *Greystok* GREYSTOKE, *holme coilram* HOLME ABBEY, *keswike* KESWICK, *kirkebee* KIRKBRIDE, *naward* NAWORTH, *penrith* PENRITH, *renglas* RAVENGLASS, *withaven* WHITEHAVEN, *Workyngton* WORKINGTON.

The O.S. 1935 misread *renglas* as Engrem. East of Carlisle, between the Eden and the Petteril, a lake is shown named *The Wathelan*. This is the mere called Ternewathelan in the Middle Ages and Tarn Wadling on the 6" Ordnance map. South of Carlisle, within a cartouche, is written *foresta de Ingelwode* INGLEWOOD FOREST. South-west of Keswick is drawn a rough indication of a mountain range and named *montes ...m...*CUMBRIAN MOUNTAINS.

DERBYSHIRE

asshbone ASHBOURNE, *Bankwell* BAKEWELL, *Castrum...* CASTLETON, *clapworth* CHARLESWORTH, *chesterfeld* CHESTERFIELD, *derbi* DERBY, *Melbourne* MELBOURNE.

Ashbourne is wrongly sited on the west bank of the Dove. North of Castleton are two circles, one within the other, round which is written *Puteus Pek.* This refers to Peak Cavern. It appears on the Matthew Paris map as an inscription 'Eolus Puteus Ventorum' and a note in the British Museum reproduction of the Matthew Paris maps published in 1928 points out that this 'marvel of Britain' is referred to in Henry of Huntingdon's *Historia Anglorum* written in the twelfth century. '*Quatuor autem sunt, quae mira videntur in Anglia. Primum quidem est, quod ventus egreditur de cavernis terrae in monte qui vocatur Pec, tanto vigore, ut vestes injectas repellat et in altum elevatas procul ejiciat.*'

LANCASHIRE

kartmell CARTMEL, *clederhowe* CLITHEROE, *cokersand* COCKERSAND ABBEY, *fournes* FURNESS,

*k..ow...*KNOWSLEY, *lancastre* LANCASTER, *lverpole* LIVERPOOL, *manches...* MANCHESTER, *prescot* PRESCOT, *preston* PRESTON, *w...ington* WARRINGTON, *...ig...* WIGAN, *wynwyke* WINWICK.

O.S. 1935 interpreted *k...ow...* as Stowe, and *kartmell* as Kermell. West of Wigan is a town with an indecipherable name that could be BURSCOUGH. Between Lancaster and Preston, within a cartouche, is written *Aundernes*, referring to the district or hundred of Amoundernes as shown on Speed's map of 1610. Off the coast at Cockersand is an island upon which something is written, but only the consecutive letters *...bre* can be read. This may refer to HILBRE ISLAND off the Wirral peninsula.

SHROPSHIRE

briggenorth BRIDGNORTH, *clun* CLUN, *ellesmere* ELLESMERE, *lil. . .hill* LILLESHALL, *l. . .lowe* LUDLOW, *oswestre* OSWESTRY, *Salopia* SHREWSBURY.

STAFFORDSHIRE

burton BURTON-UPON-TRENT, *lichefeld* LICHFIELD, *Novum castrum sub lyne* NEWCASTLE-UNDER-LYME, *Stafford* STAFFORD, *stone* STONE, *tutburi* TUTBURY.

WESTMORLAND

applebee APPLEBY, *bethum* BEETHAM, *burgh c...* BROUGH, *burgham* BROUGHAM, *kirkebie kendale* KENDAL, *kirkebie lonesdale* KIRKBY LONSDALE, *pendragon* PENDRAGON CASTLE, *Shap* SHAP.

North of Beetham, within a cartouche, is written *Kendale.* North of this is a lake named *Wenandremere* WINDERMERE.

ISLE OF MAN

r...hen CASTLETOWN (Rushen), *holm* PEEL (Holme). Underneath Peel is written *Insula de man.* Around the symbol for Peel there is some writing but only the consecutive letters *norw...* can be read. This is probably a note on the island's history. It was held by the Norwegians until 1270 and was seized from the Scots by Edward II in 1307.

FIGURE 17
Cheshire, Cumberland, Derbyshire, Lancashire, Shropshire, Staffordshire, Westmorland, and Isle of Man.

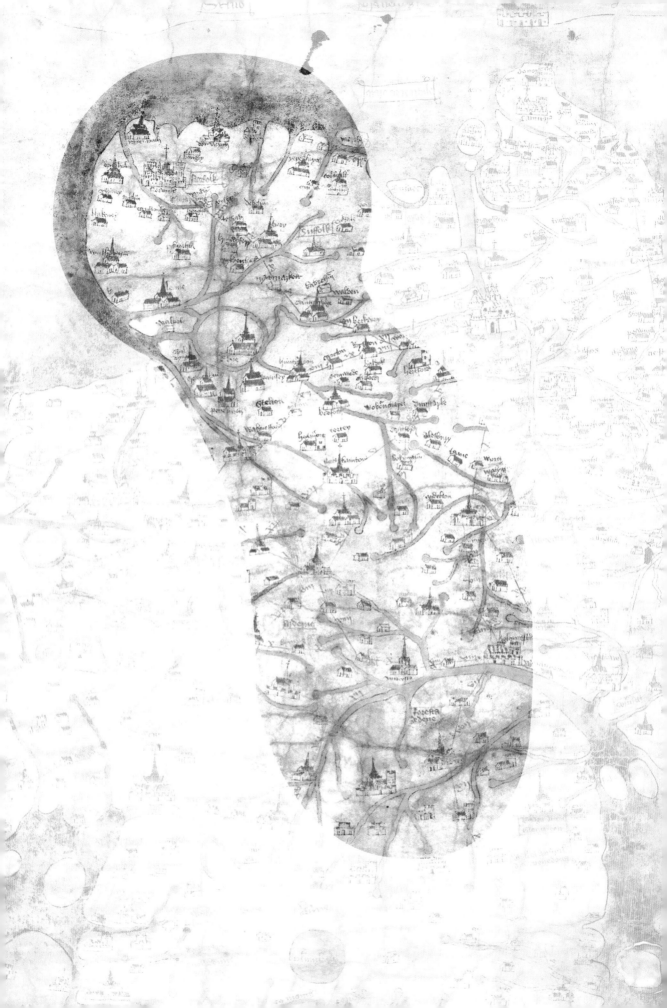

BEDFORDSHIRE

bedford BEDFORD, *dunstaple* DUNSTABLE, *sheford* SHEFFORD, *tortey* TURVEY, *wobornchapel* WOBURN. O.S. 1875 misread *sheford* as Stretford. Gough queried *tortey* as Towcester, but Towcester is now readable to the south-west and was correctly shown by the O.S. 1935.

BUCKINGHAMSHIRE

alesbury AYLESBURY, *bokyngham* BUCKINGHAM, *colbrok* COLNBROOK, *stratford* FENNY STRATFORD, *wycombe* HIGH WYCOMBE.
Gough lists Worth under his Buckinghamshire towns, but this is Tetsworth in Oxfordshire. The *worth* part of the name has been overwritten, but the *tets* can be seen under ultra-violet light. Colnbrook is placed on the east bank of the Colne instead of the west bank.

CAMBRIDGESHIRE

babreham BABRAHAM, *Cantebrege* CAMBRIDGE, *caxton* CAXTON, *Elye* ELY.

HEREFORDSHIRE

Clifford CLIFFORD, *hereford* HEREFORD, *Wigmore* WIGMORE.

HUNTINGDONSHIRE

huntyngton HUNTINGDON, *ogerston* OGERSTON, *Ramsey* RAMSEY, *seint nede* ST NEOTS, *Stelton* STILTON.

LEICESTERSHIRE

aschby ASHBY DE LA ZOUCH, *bevoir* BELVOIR, *leycestre* LEICESTER, *lo...hh...* LOUGHBOROUGH, *harborowe* MARKET HARBOROUGH, *melton* MELTON MOWBRAY.

NORFOLK

atylborow ATTLEBOROUGH, *aylesham* AYLSHAM, *blakeney* BLAKENEY, *Brumholm* BROOMHOLM, *burndon* BURNHAM, *causton* CAWSTON, *crowmere* CROMER, *derham* EAST DEREHAM, *hengham* HINGHAM, *lenne* KING'S LYNN, *Norwich* NORWICH, *pykyngham* PICKENHAM, *tetford* THETFORD, *walpole* WALPOLE, *walsyngham* WALSINGHAM, *wyndham* WYMONDHAM,

FIGURE 18
Bedfordshire, Buckinghamshire, Cambridgeshire, Herefordshire, Huntingdonshire, Leicestershire, Norfolk, Northamptonshire, Rutland, Suffolk, Warwickshire, and Worcestershire.

yernemouth YARMOUTH.
The town symbol for Wyndham has disappeared. South of Norwich, within a cartouche, is written the county name *Norfolk.*

NORTHAMPTONSHIRE

bracle BRACKLEY, *kat...by* CATESBY, *dauentre* DAVENTRY, *hegham* HIGHAM FERRERS, *Northamton* NORTHAMPTON, *towcestre* TOWCESTER, *petreburgh* PETERBOROUGH, *Rokyngham* ROCKINGHAM, *Walmesford* WANSFORD. O.S. 1935 has misread *Rokyngham* as Pakyngham.

RUTLAND

okham OAKHAM.

SUFFOLK

brandofery BRANDON, *bongay* BUNGAY, *bery* BURY ST EDMUNDS, *catiwad* CATTAWADE, *clare* CLARE, *debeham* DEBENHAM, *donwych* DUNWICH, *...xtow* FELIXSTOWE, *yepeswych* IPSWICH, *myldenhal* MILDENHALL, *nywmarkett* NEWMARKET, *orford* ORFORD, *Stratford* STRATFORD ST ANDREW.
Just east of Clare, within a cartouche, is written the county name *Suffolk.*

WARWICKSHIRE

al...tre ALCESTER, *bermyngham* BIRMINGHAM, *colshill* COLESHILL, *combe* COMBE ABBEY, *coventr...* COVENTRY, *solly..,* SOLIHULL, *...tford* STRATFORD-ON-AVON, *Warwick* WARWICK.
O.S. 1935 interpreted Coventry as Tamworth. West of Coleshill, within a cartouche, is the name *Arderne* ARDEN.

WORCESTERSHIRE

...wych DROITWICH, *evesham* EVESHAM, *k...mini...* KIDDERMINSTER, *wircestre* WORCESTER.
East of Droitwich is a town with an indecipherable name which is probably BROMSGROVE. By the side of Droitwich is written *Hic fit sal.*

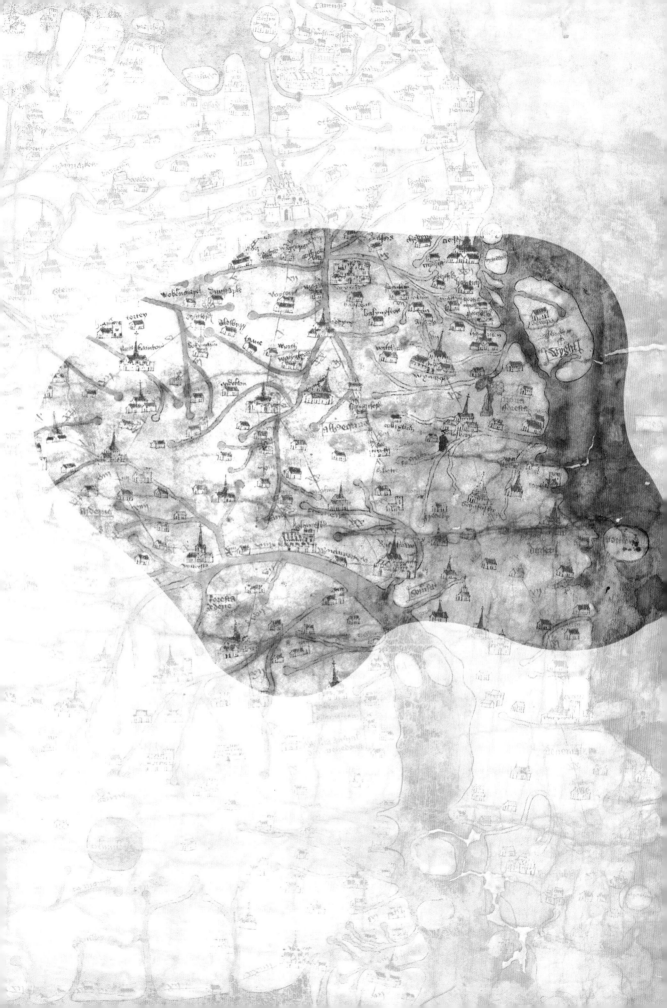

BERKSHIRE

abyngton ABINGDON, *faryngdon* FARINGDON, *hongreford* HUNGERFORD, *lamborn* LAMBOURN, *maydehed* MAIDENHEAD, *neube* NEWBURY, *redyng* READING, *walynford* WALLINGFORD, *wynsor* WINDSOR.

The *mayde* of Maydehed was seen by Gough and Sanders but the ending *hed* written underneath *mayde* has now been seen under ultra-violet light.

Wallingford is placed on the Oxfordshire side of the Thames but this, I think, is because there is no room for it on the Berkshire side. The same applies to Maidenhead. Within a cartouche is written *albus equus* VALE OF THE WHITE HORSE.

DORSETSHIRE

bridport BRIDPORT, *corffe* CORFE, *dorcest* DORCHESTER, *lyme* LYME REGIS, *pole* POOLE, *schaftisbry* SHAFTESBURY, *sherbourn* SHERBORNE, *weymothe* WEYMOUTH, *wimb...* WIMBORNE MINSTER.

North of Corfe is a town with an indecipherable name which is probably BLANDFORD. The symbol indicating the location of Sherborne has been almost obliterated and was omitted from the O.S. 1935. Off the coast at Weymouth there is an island named *portland*. West of Dorchester, within a cartouche, is written the county name *dorset*.

GLOUCESTERSHIRE

Bristowe BRISTOL, *...lteham* CHELTENHAM, *camden* CHIPPING CAMPDEN, *cicestre* CIRENCESTER, *gloucestre* GLOUCESTER, *h...les* HAILES, *newent* NEWENT, *newport* NEWPORT, *nor...lech* NORTHLEACH, *teukesbr...* TEWKESBURY.

The symbol for Cheltenham has almost disappeared, and did not appear on the O.S. 1935. The O.S. 1935 had *...don* for Camden, but the whole name is visible under ultra-violet light. North of Newent is the drawing of two trees labelled *foresta de dene* FOREST OF DEAN. This is wrongly sited: it should be to the south of Newent. The symbol for the forest has almost disappeared and was not shown on the O.S. 1935.

HAMPSHIRE

alford ALRESFORD, *alton* ALTON, *Basyngstok*

BASINGSTOKE, *bewley* BEAULIEU, *waltham* BISHOP'S WALTHAM, *botley* BOTLEY, *crist...* CHRISTCHURCH, *for...ngbrigg* FORDINGBRIDGE, *haventre* HAVANT, *lim...ton* LYMINGTON, *petrefeld* PETERSFIELD, *porchestre* PORTCHESTER, *portismouth* PORTSMOUTH, *rusey* ROMSEY, *hampton* SOUTHAMPTON, *witchirch* WHITCHURCH, *wynchestre* WINCHESTER.

North of Christchurch is a drawing of two trees labelled *Nova Foresta*. Off the coast at Havant are two small unnamed islands, probably Portsea and Hayling. Southampton is on the wrong bank of the Itchen.

ISLE OF WIGHT

carsbrok CARISBROOKE, *Newport* NEWPORT.

West of Carisbrooke, within a cartouche, is written the name of the island *Wyght*.

MONMOUTHSHIRE

bergene ABERGAVENNY, *karleon* CAERLEON, *kaerwent* CAERWENT, *chepstow* CHEPSTOW, *ebw* EBBW VALE, *m...mouth* MONMOUTH, *Newport* NEWPORT, *uske* USK.

Caerleon and Newport are sited on the east instead of the west bank of the Usk.

OXFORDSHIRE

banbery BANBURY, *burford* BURFORD, *norton* CHIPPING NORTON, *midelton* MIDDLETON STONEY, *oxonia* OXFORD, *tetsworth* TETSWORTH, *tame* THAME, *whitney* WITNEY, *Wodstok* WOODSTOCK.

The *worth* of Tetsworth has been overwritten.

WILTSHIRE

ames... AMESBURY, *calne* CALNE, *cheppenham* CHIPPENHAM, *colligborn* COLLINGBOURNE, *krykelaith* CRICKLADE, *malmesbury* MALMESBURY, *merleb...* MARLBOROUGH, *salesbery* SALISBURY, *...haven* UPAVON, *warm...* WARMINSTER. The symbol for Upavon has almost disappeared and was not given on O.S. 1935.

FIGURE 19

Berkshire, Dorset, Gloucestershire, Hampshire, Isle of Wight, Monmouthshire, Oxfordshire, and Wiltshire.

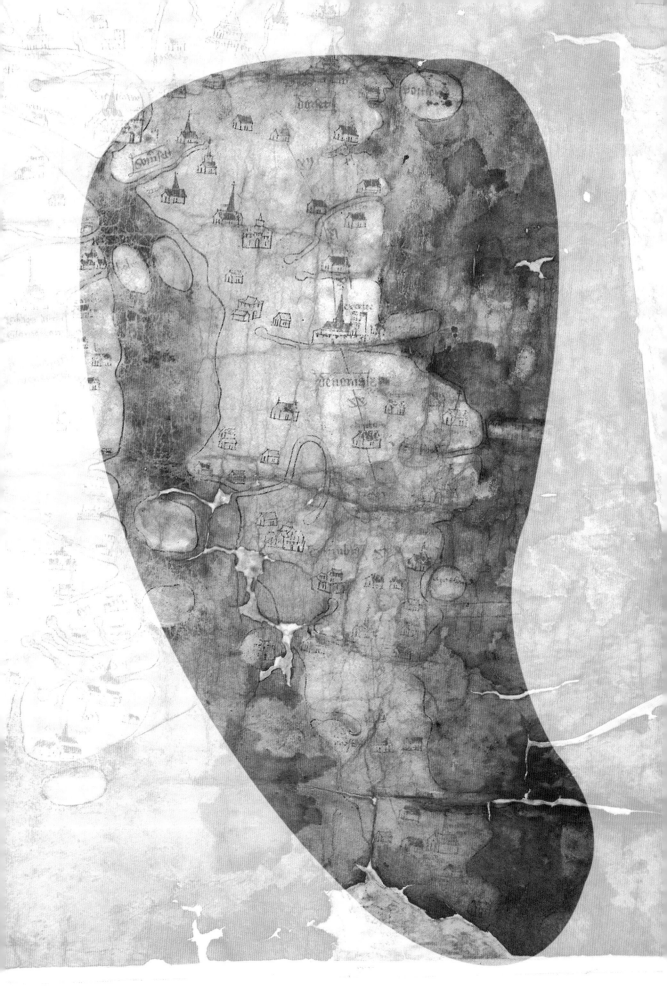

CORNWALL

...m... BODMIN, boscast... BOSCASTLE, camelford
CAMELFORD, fowy FOWEY, lisk... LISKEARD, looe
LOOE, l...w... LOSTWITHIEL, padstow PADSTOW, pens...
PENZANCE, ...ruth REDRUTH, seint b...
ST BURYAN, s...n...c...mb ST COLUMB, ...man
ST GERMANS, Iwes ST IVES, mons mich...
ST MICHAEL'S MOUNT, ...ony TREGONY,
...ew... TRURO.

West of Lostwithiel is a town with an indecipherable name
which I have not been able to identify. Off the coast near
Boscastle is an island upon which stands a castle. The name
is indecipherable, but it must be TINTAGEL. North of
Liskeard is a town on the road from Launceston to
Camelford with an indecipherable name. North-east of
Camelford and just to the west of the name *Cornubia* is a
fairly large town with an indecipherable name. It might be
STRATTON. From Okehampton a distance figure *xvi* is
given and beyond a particularly badly creased portion of
the map another distance figure *xx*.

I suspect that the town of Launceston was originally shown
between these two distance figures. The bridge shown over
the river near Camelford is the Wadebridge. South of
Tregony there is some writing on the peninsula of which
mene... can be read. This is probably MENEAGE. North-
west of Bodmin is a hill symbol which possibly refers to
Bodmin Moor. South of Liskeard is an island called
motland. This is now ST GEORGE'S ISLAND or LOOE
ISLAND. To the west of Motland is a label which was
noted by Sanders, who stated that it 'has never borne the
inscription intended for it'. Ultra-violet light has revealed
that there is an inscription, but it is indecipherable except
for the consecutive letters *magna*. Off St Buryan is an island
named *Celly* SCILLY ISLANDS. The county name
Cornubia is placed within a cartouche just east of what
might be Stratton.

DEVONSHIRE

aschperton ASHBURTON, *ba...stab...* BARNSTAPLE,
b...ford BIDEFORD, *chim...* CHULMLEIGH, *coliford*
COLYFORD, *dertemouth* DARTMOUTH, *exceter*
EXETER, *exm...* EXMOUTH, *h...* HARTLAND,
honyton HONITON, *combe* ILFRACOMBE, *okinton*
OKEHAMPTON, *plymouth* PLYMOUTH, *t...ok*
TAVISTOCK, *teverton* TIVERTON, *totnes* TOTNES.

FIGURE 20
Cornwall, Devon, and Somerset.

South-east of Barnstaple is a town with a name which
might be MOLTON. East of Ilfracombe are two towns
with indecipherable names. These could be COMBE
MARTIN and LYNTON. North-west of Dartmouth is a
circle in which is written *dertesmour* DARTMOOR. Off the
coast at Dartmouth is a label in which is written *hic Brutus
applicuit cum Troianis*. This refers to the legendary invasion of
Albion which King Edward I in his letter of 7 May 1301 to
Pope Boniface claiming the Kingdom of Scotland mentions:
'*Sub temporibus itaque Ely & Samuelis Prophetae, vir quidam strenuus
& insignis, Brutus nomine, degenere Trojanorum, post excidium urbis
Trojae, cummultis nobilibus Trojanorum, applicuit in quandam insulam,
tunc Albion vocatam, a gigantibus inhabitatam: quibus sua & suorum
devictis potentia & occisis, eam nomine suo Britanniam, sociosque suos
Britones appellavit; & aedificavit civitatemquam Trinovantum
nuncupavit, quae modo Londonia nominatur.*' South of Exeter and
Exmouth a peninsula is drawn upon which writing can be
seen. Only the word *chekstones* can be read. This refers to a
sandbank or shoal in the mouth of the Exe. It is shown and
named on Saxton's map of Devon, 1575. West of Exeter,
within a cartouche is written the county name *devonia*. Off
the north coast is an island upon which can be read *...undy*
LUNDY.

SOMERSETSHIRE

axbrig axbridge, *br...gw...* bridgwater, *chard* CHARD, *gl...*
GLASTONBURY, *...ton* TAUNTON, *Uphill* UPHILL.
The other towns of Somersetshire are indecipherable.
North of Tiverton is possibly DUNSTER and east of
Dunster CLEEVE ABBEY. Twelve miles by the road from
Chard is either CREWKERNE or YEOVIL with
ILCHESTER to the north. Between Bristol and
Shaftesbury are three towns, possibly WELLS, FROME,
and BRUTON. North of Axbridge, within a cartouche,
is the county name *Somerset*. Off the north coast are two
islands and upon each is written *holm*. These are
FLATHOLM and STEEPHOLM.

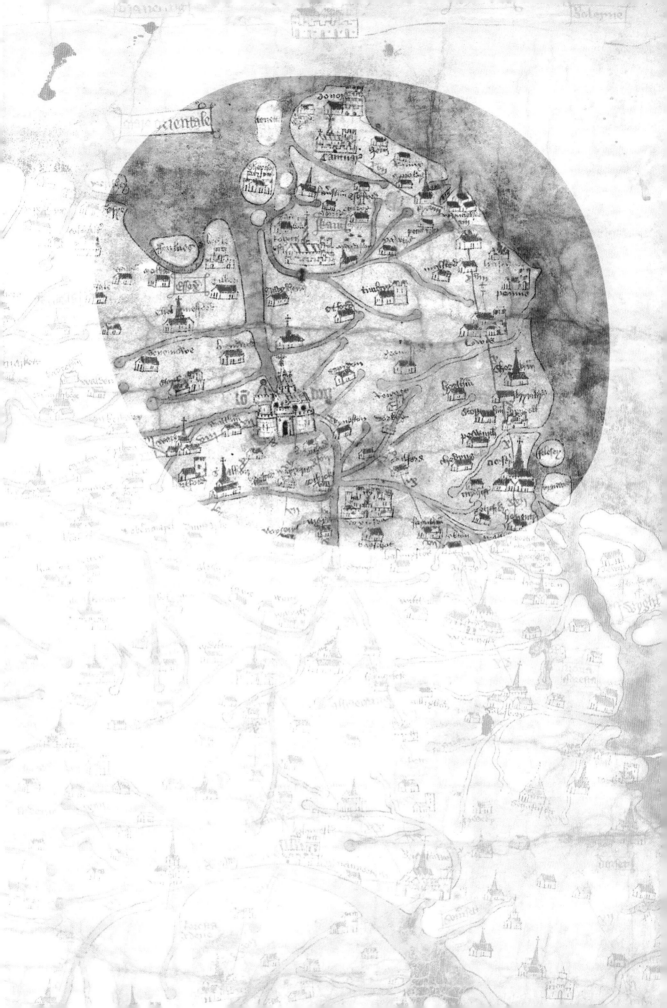

ESSEX

brantr... BRAINTREE, *brendwod* BRENTWOOD, *Chelmesford* CHELMSFORD, *Coksale* COGGESHALL, *colchestre* COLCHESTER, *donemowe* GREAT DUNMOW, *hadle* HADLEIGH, *...wich* HARWICH, *maldon* MALDON, *walden* SAFFRON WALDEN, *s. osye* ST OSYTH, *Tilberi* TILBURY, *waltham* WALTHAM ABBEY, *witham* WITHAM. Harwich is placed on the wrong bank of the Stour. Off the coast by Maldon is an island named *Foulnes* FOULNESS, and off St Osyth another named *mereshey* MERSEA. Between Maldon and Tilbury within a cartouche is written the county name *Essex.*

HERTFORDSHIRE

Baldok BALDOCK, *berkwey* BARKWAY, *barnet* BARNET, *stortford* BISHOP'S STORTFORD, *hertford* HERTFORD, *Royston* ROYSTON, *S. albon* ST ALBANS, *ware* WARE, *boreford* WATFORD.

Gough misread *stortford* as Romford.

KENT

appeldre APPLEDORE, *ashford* ASHFORD, *Cantuar'* CANTERBURY, *cheryng* CHARING, *dertford* DARTFORD, *dovor* DOVER, *fevarsham* FAVERSHAM, *graveshend* GRAVESEND, *heth* HYTHE, *maideston* MAIDSTONE, *ospring* OSPRINGE, *otford* OTFORD, *Rowchestr* ROCHESTER, *Rumy* ROMNEY, *sandwych* SANDWICH, *sithingborn* SITTINGBOURNE, *tunbryg* TONBRIDGE, *yawhour* YALDING.

The name Cheryng appears twice in different handwriting. The original forms of Heth, Rumy, and Appeldre have been overwritten in another hand and Yawhour has been written over Yaldy. Between Charing and Maidstone is a semicircle of small roundish marks and something has been written just to the east of it which is indecipherable. It may be connected with the town of Leeds with its castle and abbey. Between Rye and Appledore is a circular symbol: this may refer to Oxney Island. A bridge is shown over the Medway west of Rochester. Off the north coast are three unnamed islands, probably Grain, Elmley, and Harty, and beyond them another island, with a large castle named *Shephey* SHEPPEY. Sheppey castle was entirely rebuilt in the reign of Edward III and in 1366 its name was changed to Queenborough in honour of his queen Philippa. East of Sheppey is another island named *tenett* THANET. East of Rochester, within a cartouche, is written the county name *Kant.*

MIDDLESEX

braynford BRENTFORD, *london* LONDON, *Waxsbrigg* UXBRIDGE.

SURREY

bagschot BAGSHOT, *chedyngfold* CHIDDINGFOLD, *cobham* COBHAM, *croidon* CROYDON, *dorkyng* DORKING, *farnham* FARNHAM, *Gilford* GUILDFORD, *kyngston* KINGSTON, *Reigate* REIGATE.

The *chedynd* of Chedyngfold has been written in a later hand.

SUSSEX

arundell ARUNDEL, *ba...le* BATTLE, *borham* BOREHAM STREET, *brymbre* BRAMBER, *cicestre* CHICHESTER, *grenested* EAST GRINSTEAD, *hastynges* HASTINGS, *horsham* HORSHAM, *lewes* and *Lewis* LEWES, *malsted* MAYFIELD, *mydhest* MIDHURST, *petwurth* PETWORTH, *peuins* PEVENSEY, *pons robt.* ROBERTSBRIDGE, *Rye* RYE, *Shoreham* SHOREHAM, *Stopham* STOPHAM, *Wynchelsee* WINCHELSEA.

Malsted is written in a later hand over Marfeld. Lewes appears in different hands as Lewes and Lewis. Off the coast at Chichester are two islands named *selesey* SELSEY and *manwod* MANHOOD. Selsey is shown as an island and Manhope as a peninsula named The Manhoed on Mercator's map of 1564.

FIGURE 21
Essex, Hertfordshire, Kent, Middlesex, Surrey, and Sussex.

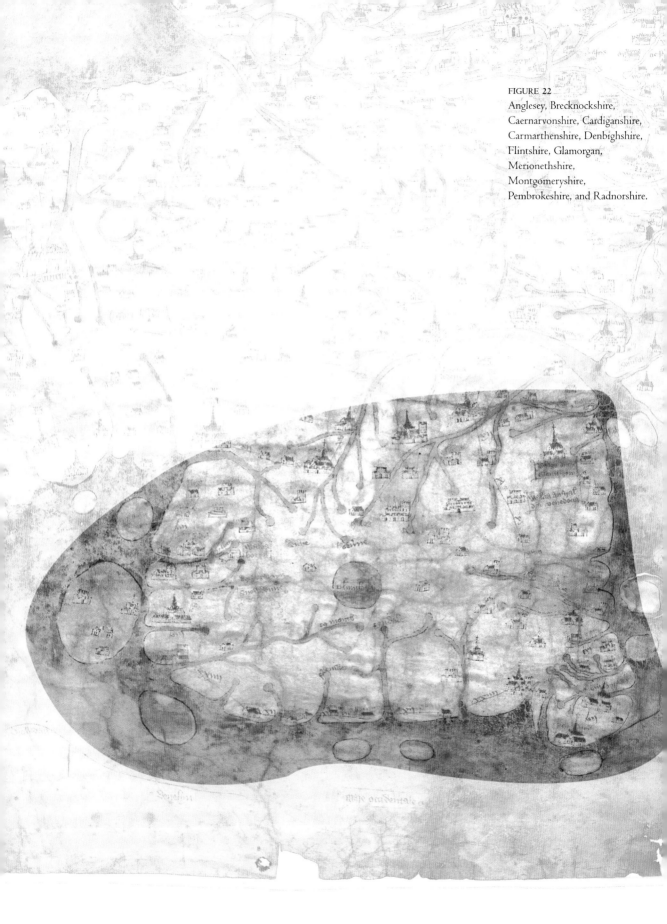

FIGURE 22
Anglesey, Brecknockshire,
Caernarvonshire, Cardiganshire,
Carmarthenshire, Denbighshire,
Flintshire, Glamorgan,
Merionethshire,
Montgomeryshire,
Pembrokeshire, and Radnorshire.

ANGLESEY

aberfraw ABERFFRAW, *beaumorres* BEAUMARIS, *lanvar* LLANFAES, *...nka...l...* LLANGADWALADR.

On the island is written *Insula de Anglesey habens xxiiij mil. in long, et xviij in lat.* Beaumaris is wrongly sited in the north, and just east of Aberfraw is a long name of which a few letters are visible. These letters and the location would indicate that the place is Llangadwaladr. To the east of Anglesey is another island upon which is written *prestisle* PRESTHOLM.

BRECKNOCKSHIRE

brekenok BRECON, *lowell* LLYWEL.

CAERNARVONSHIRE

bangor BANGOR, *kaernarvan* CAERNARVON, *conw...* CONWAY, *crykkey* CRICCIETH, *tulbadern* DOLBADARN. Eight miles south-west of Conway and fifteen south-east of Bangor is a town on the Ogwen with an indecipherable name. It could well be CAPEL CURIG. SNOWDON is shown as a hill and labelled *Snowdonne.* Off the coast is BARDSEY ISLAND upon which is written *Bardesey ubi sunt britonum vaticinatores.* There are also two smaller islands upon which can be read *...l...n* and *...well.* These I take to be GWYLAN and ST TUDWAL'S ISLAND although they are shown off Aberystwyth.

CARDIGANSHIRE

Aberestwyth ABERYSTWYTH, *kardigan* CARDIGAN, *...beder* LAMPETER, *lanmihangel* LLANFIHANGEL CASTELL GWALLTER, *...ratflo...* STRATA FLORIDA, *...wyth* YSPYTTY YSTWYTH.

North-east of Lampeter is a town with an indecipherable name which I take to be TREGARON. Its location with regard to Landury and Lampeter is about right. The river Teifi is omitted, and Cardigan stands on an inlet. Plynlimon is shown by a circle through which is drawn wavy lines as if it were a lake and named *Plimilemon.* To the southeast of Plynlimon is the drawing of a range of mountains, scarcely visible, omitted from the O.S. 1935 reproduction.

CARMARTHENSHIRE

carmar... CARMARTHEN, *k...l..y* KIDWELLY, *land...l...* LLANDEILO, *landury* LLANDOVERY, *lan...dok* LLANGADOG, *saint clears* ST CLEARS, *t...l...hay* TALLEY, *Whitland* WHITLAND.

DENBIGHSHIRE

aberkele ABERGELE, *dynbe* DENBIGH, *...ther...* GWYTHERIN, *Ruthyn* RUTHIN.

A town south of Ruthin and between the rivers Dee and Clwyd is clearly named *Engan,* but I think DINAS BRAN near Llangollen is intended. In the middle of the county within a cartouche are the words *Wallia borealis.*

FLINTSHIRE

hawarden HAWARDEN, *flynt* FLINT, *orton* OVERTON, *rudland* RHUDDLAN, *Ste asaph* ST ASAPH.

GLAMORGANSHIRE

kardyf CARDIFF, *coubrigge* COWBRIDGE, *ewanye* EWENNY, *landaf* LLANDAFF, *landor* LLANDOW, *loghor* LOUGHOR, *margam* MARGAM, *Neath* NEATH, *swansee* SWANSEA. O.S. 1935 has read *kardyf* as Caphyl. West of Swansea is a town with an indecipherable name that could be LLANDDEWI or possibly PENRICE. There are two descriptive labels: one reads *Plaga dicta Glamorgan* and the other *Wallia australis dicta venedocia.*

MERIONETHSHIRE

aberduwrey ABERDOVEY, *abermaw* BARMOUTH, *harlech* HARLECH, *...towyn* LLANENDDWYN.

The Dovey is wrongly named – it should be the Maw or Month – and the *Ridale* is really the Dovey.

MONTGOMERYSHIRE

loge

Loge could possibly be intended for Llanllugan, the site of an ancient Cistercian nunnery founded in 1239 – but this would place it beyond the Severn. The town should be somewhere near Montgomery or might even be intended for that town. North-east of Plynlimon is a town with an indecipherable name which could be YSTRAD MARCHELL.

PEMBROKESHIRE

dale DALE, *havford* HAVERFORDWEST, *l...haythyn* LLAWHADEN, *newport* NEWPORT, *pembrok* PEMBROKE, *sent david* ST DAVID'S, *tynbey* TENBY. Off the west coast is an island named *Ramesey* RAMSEY and off the south coast is another named *calday* CALDY.

RADNORSHIRE

Clero CLYRO, *c...pa...* PAINSCASTLE, *prest...gn...* PRESTEIGNE, *rad...* RADNOR. Midway between Radnor and Llandovery is another town with the name obliterated. I find this impossible to identify.

The following names do not appear as part of mainland Britain.

CHANNEL ISLANDS
Five islands are shown and all are named.

...dern... ALDERNEY.

Sark SARK.

Gernesey GUERNSEY. *Gernesey* is written within a cartouche and there are two town symbols. The one on the east has the letters *castr* readable. This might be CASTLE CORNET. The one to the south has an indecipherable name. There is other indecipherable writing on the island.

Ancrowe. This probably refers to the ECHREHOU ISLANDS.

Gersey JERSEY. One town symbol is shown on the island and of its name the letters *h...y* can be read. This is ST HELIER, or St Hillary as Speed's map has it.

OTHER NAMES OUTSIDE GREAT BRITAIN
The eastern coast of Ireland is shown with four names: *Stranford* STRANGFORD, *Carlenford* CARLINGFORD, *Drowdaa* DROGHEDA, *Develyn* DUBLIN.

To the east a coast line is shown with the names *Norway*, *Dacia* DENMARK, *Sklus* SLUIS, *Graveling* GRAVELINES, *Caleys* CALAIS, *Whitsand* WISSANT, *Boleyne* BOLOGNE. Calais is the only one with a vignette of the town.

Between northern England and the Danish coasts the North Sea is labelled *Mare aquilonare sine termino* and off the Thames *Mare Orientale.* The English Channel between the south coast and the Channel Islands is labelled *Mare Australe.*

The Irish Sea between south-east Ireland and Wales is labelled *Mare Occidental.*

Insula de Orkenoy

cominga
de aleyn

comynga
de Tosta

comynga
de nayn

comynga
de nayn

vbenis

ago in þe tonn
þ veyanþ passag

out of
towne

comynga
de fyf

comynga
de locherire

comynga
de cortus

comynga
de
Gothelond

fön
sognoty
laga

comynga de
Gothelond

þlaga de Tingwall

golaynge
breynzeyn
zoriens

þlaga de kyngeþ

comynga de Tuedale

les out yſles

RIVERS

Tributaries are listed under the main river. An asterisk indicates that the name is indecipherable.

twede TWEED

fl Edre BLACKADDER

fl teviot

fl *JED WATER Identified from the position of Jedburgh. The tributary on the right bank east of Wark is probably the *TILL.

*ALN Identified from the position of Bolton and Alnwick.

*COQUET. Identified from the position of Felton and other towns on its banks.

fl wanspek WANSBECK

fl nortyne NORTH TYNE

fl southtyne SOUTH TYNE

fl Were WEAR

fl tese TEES

fl gretay GRETA

Humbre HUMBER

fl derwent

fl rie RYE

fl ouse

fl swale

fl yore URE

fl skyl SKELL

fl nyd NIDD

fl warf WHARFE

The tributary on the left bank between Hull and Beverley is probably the *HULL RIVER.

The position of Pontefract would make the tributary on the right bank the *AIRE.

fl de trent TRENT

fl done DON

fl sore SOAR

The tributary which passes through Blyth could be the *RYTON and the other between Mattersey and Torksey could be the *IDLE.

The tributary *DERWENT passing through Derby and its own tributary *WYE are shown embracing the Peak.

The tributary of the Derwent shown at Ashbourne is an error. It should be part of the *DOVE which is rightly shown joining the Trent near Tutbury. The tributary

between Stone and Stafford could be the *SOW although Stafford is shown on the wrong bank. The tributary from Lichfield to Birmingham could be the *TAME although Lichfield would then be misplaced.

fl ankeholyn ANCHOLME

fl witham

fl welland

*NENE This is shown as a tributary of the Welland.

*GREAT OUSE This river is shown with its tributaries *TOVE, *OUZEL, *IVEL, *CAM, *LARK, and *LITTLE OUSE.

fl braydyng YARE

The tributary *TUD is shown with Dereham on its bank.

*ALDE Identified from Orford at its mouth and Stratford St. Andrew upon its bank.

*DEBEN Identified from Debenham near its source.

*STOUR Identified from Cattawade Bridge. The river should continue across Suffolk to Clare.

fl tamys THAMES

fl charwell CHERWELL

fl kene KENNET

The tributary whose source is north of Dunmow and which enters the Thames east of Brentwood would seem to be the *CHELMER, *WID, and *MAR DYKE wrongly connected to form one river. The tributary on which Bishop's Stortford stands seems to be a combination of the *STORT and the *RODING. The next westwards on the north bank is the *LEA which runs through Ware with its own tributary the *RIB which passes near Barkway. The *BRENT is identified from Brentford; the *COLNE from its junction with the Thames at Colnbrook; the *WYE from High Wycombe; the *THAME from Thame; the *EVENLODE from Woodstock; and the *WINDRUSH from Burford. On the right bank the tributary joining the Thames at Cricklade is probably the *SWILL BROOK. The Kennet is named but the branch which joins it at Newbury is the *LAMBOURN. The tributary joining the Thames at Reading is probably the *LODDON, Basingstoke being sited on the wrong bank. East of Windsor the *WEY is shown passing through Guildford;

and the *MOLE with Cobham and Dorking on its banks. The tributary between Cobham and Kingston is probably the *HOGSWILL RIVER, and that from Croydon to London the *WANDLE. East of the Wandle is probably the *RAVENSBOURNE and finally the *DARENT upon which stands Dartford.

fl med... MEDWAY
The western branch at Yalding is probably the *TEISE and the eastern branch the *BEULT. The branch at Maidstone is probably the *LEN. Robertsbridge is shown on the Beult, but this has been confused with the *ROTHER which flows into the sea at Rye.
*GREAT STOUR. Identified from its position in relation to Canterbury and Ashford.

——— ENGLAND AND WALES – WEST COAST FROM NORTH TO SOUTH ———

fl eden
fl irthyng IRTHING
fl caldew
fl ...erell PETTERIL
The tributary upon which Penrith stands is probably the *EAMONT with the *LOWTHER shown to the west of Shap. East of Shap is probably the *LYVENNET.
*WAVER Identified from Holme Abbey.
*DERWENT This is probably the river Derwent with its tributary the *COCKER – shown embracing Cockermouth.
*EHEN The river just south of Whitehaven is probably the Ehen.
esk
doden DUDDON
leven
Kent
lon LUNE
fl rybell RIBBLE
fl Mersee MERSEY
*DEE Identified from Chester on its bank.
The tributary whose source is shown near Oswestry is probably the *CEIRIOG
fl clotte CLWYD
I cannot identify the tributary.
fl ogwayn OGWEN
I cannot identify the tributaries.
fl saint SEIONT This is shown passing just to the west of Bangor as on Mercator's map, but it really passes to the west of Caernarvon.

fl month This is shown with Caernarvon on the east bank of its estuary, i.e. in the position of the Seiont. Dolbadarn is also shown on the eastern bank which means that the compiler was showing the course of the Seiont. The upper reaches of the supposed river

are confused with the Mawddach (called the Moth by Saxton), and given the name Month. The river also is shown on the Lily map as Moith and on Mercator as Month.
*DWYFAWR The river north of Criccieth could be the Dwyfawr.
*GLASLYN The river between Harlech and Criccieth could be the Glaslyn.
fl douwrey DOVEY This is really the MAWDDACH.
fl ridale RHEIDOL This is really the Dovey and the town on the north of the estuary is Aberdovey.
I cannot identify the names of the tributaries of the Rheidol.
*YSTWYTH The river north of Cardigan is the Ystwyth, the distance is given as 24 miles and this brings us to Aberystwyth which in fact is the name given on the north of the estuary.
The estuary at Cardigan is that of the Teifi, but the river is not shown.
*WEST CLEDDAU Identified from the position of Haverfordwest.
fl clethy EAST CLEDDAU
The tributary is probably the *SYFYNWY.
*TAF Identified from the position of St. Clears on its bank.

fl ...wy TYWI (TOWY)
The tributary *GWILI which joins the main river at Carmarthen is confused in its upper reaches with the Teifi.
*TAFF The river to the west of Cardiff could be the Taff.
fl uske USK
The tributary which joins the main river at Caerleon is probably the *AVON-LWYD.
fl wye The Wye is shown to the south instead of the

north of Clifford and its source is shown just south of Painscastle instead of Plynlimon.

fl log LUGG The compiler has confused the Teme, a tributary of the Severn, with the Lugg. Ludlow is on the Teme, and Clun on its tributary the Clun. The Lugg should flow south of Wigmore and north of Presteigne.

fl dyveles DYVELES This may be the SUMMERGIL BROOK called Wadels fl. on Saxton's map of Hereford.

fl severne SEVERN

The tributary south of Newent is possibly the *LEADON.

The tributary opposite Worcester is the *TEME with its course wrongly shown east of Ludlow.

The other tributaries on the right bank are impossible to identify.

Left bank tributaries:

fl worfe WORFE

fl salw... SALWARPE This flows between Droitwich and Bromsgrove and the tributary shown is probably *ELMLEY BROOK.

fl avon This river is shown as having Ashby and Coventry on its banks as well as Warwick and Stratford. The tributary upon which Alcester stands is the *ARROW.

The tributary on the left bank is the *ISBOURNE.

fl avon This is the Bristol Avon with two unidentified tributaries.

*AXE The river between Bristol and Uphill is probably the Axe with Axbridge on the right bank. In this case Uphill has been wrongly sited on the left bank.

*TORRIDGE The next river shown west of the Axe is probably the Torridge. The name is indecipherable. Something is written across the river but only the letter *h* can be read. It could be *fl Torighe*, the form used in the Close Rolls in 1371.

ENGLAND AND WALES – SOUTH COAST FROM WEST TO EAST

The river shown from Boscastle past Camelford to the English Channel is in its upper reaches possibly part of the Camel, but it is impossible to say what the rest of it is supposed to be.

*EXE Identified from the towns of Exeter and Exmouth on its banks.

*OTTER Identified from Honiton.

*AXE The river entering the sea between Colyford and Lyme is probably the Axe.

fl yoo Dorchester is shown upon this river which is difficult to see because of creases in the parchment. No river runs southwards through Dorchester to the sea although an unnamed one is shown on Mercator's map of 1564.

*STOUR The river entering the sea next to the Avon and having Wimbourne on its bank is probably the Stour.

fl avon

fl Wely WYLYE

The other tributary on the right bank could be the *NADDER and the one on the left bank the *BOURNE which joins the Avon at Salisbury and has Collingbourne on its bank.

*fl *TEST Identified from Romsey on the left bank and the position of Southampton.

*ITCHEN Identified from Winchester.

*HAMBLE The river shown between Botley and Bishop's Waltham is probably the Hamble.

*fl *ARUN Identified from Arundel.

*FL. *OUSE The name is almost readable but identified from Lewes.

ISLE OF WIGHT

fl yare YAR

SCOTLAND – EAST COAST FROM SOUTH TO NORTH

I cannot identify the river north of Coldingham.

*TYNE The river between Haddington and Hailes could be the Tyne but Haddington should be on the left bank and Hailes on the right.

*WATER OF LEITH Identified from the position of Edinburgh.

fl forth

The tributary *TEITH is shown joining a river (? Loch Lomond) flowing westwards thus cutting Scotland into two parts. The tributary on the left bank to the west of Cambuskenneth could be *ALLAN WATER. I cannot identify the river between Culross and Dunfermline.

*LEVEN Identified from Loch Leven with castle which is shown as the source.
*TAY Identified from Loch Tay.
fl erin EARN
I cannot identify the tributary between Glamis and Scone.
*ESK With Montrose and Brechin as guides the next river northwards is probably the Esk, both North and South.
*COWIE The river flowing between Cowie and Inverbervie is probably the Cowie.

fl d... Although with Aberdeen shown on the north bank this could be the Dee, there is confusion with the Don upon which Kildrummy stands and the decipherable letters could refer to either.
fl spey The names of the tributaries are indecipherable.
fl... With the castle of the earls of Ross on the north bank this could be Cromarty Firth.
I cannot identify the other rivers to the north.

SCOTLAND – WEST COAST FROM SOUTH TO NORTH

fl eske ESK
fl anant ANNAN
fl nyth NITH
fl dee I think the Bladenoch river upon which Wigtown stands is meant here and that it is shown wrongly flowing through a loch into Loch Ryan. The name could well be confused with the Cree which enters the sea three miles to the east of Wigtown. The loch has a building shown in it with an indecipherable name, but which could be Soulseat.
fl ... I cannot identify the river shown to the south of Corsewall.
fl locheriane LOCH RYAN
fl dene DOON
fl kile COYLE
aqua Clide CLYDE
The tributary on the right bank is probably *SOUTH CALDER WATER with Bothwell at the junction.

The tributary on the left bank flowing from near Douglas is probably *DOUGLAS WATER.
On the left bank opposite South Calder Water is shown what is probably *AVON WATER. The tributary south of Rutherglen could be *ROTTEN CALDER.
The river shown north of the Clyde appears to incorporate Loch Lomond and join up with the Teith, thus isolating north Scotland from the south. North of this river, and shown flowing through Lennox, is possibly Loch Long. The river south of Lorne is possibly Loch Fyne. North of the Grampians the first river could be Loch Linnhe with the islands of Iona and Mull to the West, but with the surrounding mountains it could be the sheltered waters of the Kyle of Loch Alsh used as the first stage of the journey to Lewis and the north.
The rivers shown north of this point I cannot identify.

ROADS AND DISTANCES

MAIN ROADS AND BRANCHES

1. London X Kingston V Cobham XV Guildford IX Farnham VII Alton VII Alresford VII Winchester XX Salisbury X VIII Shaftesbury XII Sherborne XX Crewkerne XII Chard XI Honiton XII Exeter XX Okehampton XVI [Launceston] XX... Camelford XV Bodmin ... St. Columb X...V St. Ives.

2. London ... Brentford XVII Colnbrook VII Maidenhead X Reading XV Newbury VII Hungerford VIII
Marlborough XXX }
Chippenham XX } Bristol

2a. Reading XX Oxford

3. London XV Uxbridge XII High Wycombe X Tetsworth X Oxford X Witney VII Burford VIII Northleach XV Gloucester VII Newent XVII Hereford XII Clyro X Brecon X Llywel XVIII Llangadock ... Llandeilo X Carmarthen ... St. Clears XI Llawhaden VIII Haverfordwest VII St. David's.

3a. Oxford XII Faringdon XX Malmesbury XX Bristol.

3b. Oxford V Abingdon.

4. London X Barnet X St Albans X Dunstable VIII Stratford ... Buckingham VI Towcester XII Daventry XVI Coventry VIII Coleshill XII Lichfield ... Stone VI Newcastle-under-Lyme XXIIII Warrington VIII Wigan XII Preston XX Lancaster XVI Kendal XX Shap ... Penrith XVI Carlisle.

4a. Stratford V Northampton XII Market Harborough XII Leicester.

4b. Stone ... Stafford.

5. London XII Waltham Abbey VIII Ware XIII Royston IX Caxton VIII Huntingdon XIIII Ogerston V Wansford V Stamford XVI Grantham X Newark X Tuxford X Blyth VIII Doncaster X Pontefract XX Wetherby VIII Boroughbridge XIIII Leeming X Gilling X Bowes XIII Brough XI Appleby X Penrith XVI Carlisle.

5a. Ware XII Barkway XII Cambridge X Newmarket X Bury St. Edmunds X Thetford XXXII Norwich.

5b. Doncaster XIII Wakefield ... Bradford ... Skipton X Settle XII Kirkby Lonsdale
VIII Kendal }
... Shap }

SECONDARY ROADS AND BRANCHES

1. Southampton ... Havant XXII Chichester X Arundel X Bramber X Lewes XVIII Boreham Street ... Battle VII Winchelsea VIII Rye ... Appledore XVII Canterbury.

2. Cardigan XXIIII Aberystwyth XII Aberdovey XII Barmouth XI Llanenddwyn ... Harlech XII Criccieth XXIIII Caernarvon VIII Bangor XV [Capel Curig] VIII Conway ... Abergele IIII Rhuddlan X Flint X Chester.

3. Bristol XV Newport XV Gloucester VIII Tewkesbury XIII Worcester X Droitwich XIIII Solihull VIII Coventry XVI Leicester X Melton Mowbray X Grantham.

3a. Droitwich X Birmingham X Lichfield XVI Derby XV Chesterfield XVI Doncaster.

3b. Worcester XII Kidderminster XII Bridgnorth XV Shrewsbury XII Ellesmere VII Overton XII Chester X Liverpool.

4. Bristol X[V?] ...

5. Bristol XIII Axbridge.

6. Richmond X Bolton X Hawes X Sedbergh X Kirkby Lonsdale.

7. Bridport X Lyme.

LOCAL ROADS – LINCOLNSHIRE

1. Lincoln XIIII Sleaford.

2. Lincoln XXVI Boston.

3. Lincoln X Spital-in-the-Street X Kirton ... Brigg VIII Barton.

4. Barton XII Caistor XVI Horncastle V Bolingbroke IX Boston.

5. Boston XII Spalding.

6. Boston XII Wainfleet.

LOCAL ROADS – YORKSHIRE

1. Leeming XII Helperby X York.

2. York XIIII Malton V Pickering.

3. York X Pocklington VII Market Weighton.

4. York XVI Market Weighton VIII Beverley.

5. York XVI Howden.

6. Beverley XVI Bridlington XII Scarborough XII Whitby XVII Guisborough.

Notes

1. E.J.S. Parsons, *The Map of Great Britain circa A.D. 1360 known as The Gough Map* (Oxford: printed for the Bodleian Library and the Royal Geographical Society by the University Press, 1958). This publication includes full listings of place names rivers and routes, and also provides a detailed analysis of the map and its history.

2. DigiData Technologies Limited <http://www.digidata.co.uk/home/digi/>.

3. Oxford Digital Library <http://www.odl.ox.ac.uk/>.

4. Andrew W. Mellon Foundation <http://www.mellon.org/>

5. Initiative announced in *Oxford University Gazette*, 16 October 2003.

6. 'Paper to Pixels: the Digital Manipulation of the Gough Map', by Rob Watts, Bournemouth University – DigiData Technologies Limited.

7. British Academy <http://www.britac.ac.uk>.

8. *Mapping the Realm: English Cartographic Construction of Fourteenth-century Britain* <http://www.qub.ac.uk/urban_mapping/gough_map/>.

9. Paul Harvey, 'Medieval Maps to 1500', Helen Wallis (gen. ed.), *Historians' Guide to Early British Maps. Royal Historical Society Guides and Handbooks*, 18 (London: Royal Historical Society, 1994), pp. 13-14.

10. R. Mason, *The Gough Map of Great Britain, 35mm colour filmstrip published by the Bodleian Library, Oxford*) – p. 2 in the pamphlet produced to accompany the filmstrip available for sale from the Bodleian Library at: <http://www.bodley.ox.ac.uk/guides/maps/films.htm>.

11. 55.3 by 116.4 cm (22 by 45 1/2 inches), with the join located 29.5 cm (11 1/2 inches) from the left-hand edge.

12. The original skin has suffered damage in several places and has been repaired. In some cases where the new vellum is visible it has been coloured green in an attempt to match the original. Fortunately the damaged areas are outside the main map outline except for small portions of the northern coasts of Cornwall and Devon, but even here no detail has been lost. The largest damaged area is a narrow strip about 20 cm (8 inches) long extending westwards from Jersey, and part of that island's coastline is missing. There are several tears along the lower edge of the map including a fairly large one off Land's End. The physical description details of the map are taken from an internal Bodleian Library conservation report, prepared in advance of the map's exhibit at Hereford Cathedral in 1999.

13. This is paralleled on Matthew Paris' maps and probably survives from an early type of World map. See, for example, the reproduction of a map of Europe accompanying a manuscript of Giraldus Cambrensis (Gerald of Wales) in John J. O'Meara, *The First Version of the Topography of Ireland* (Dundalk: Dundalgan Press, 1951).

14. W.B. Sanders, *The Thirty-second Report of the Deputy Keeper of the Public Records*, 1 (London: HMSO, 1871), pp. v-viii.

15. Catherine Delano-Smith and Roger J.P. Kain, *English Maps: a History* (London: British Library, 1999), p. 47.

16. Parsons, *The Map of Great Britain*, 2nd. edn., p. 2.

17. Daniel Birkholz, *The King's Two Maps: Cartography and Culture in Thirteenth-century England* (London: Routledge, 2004), p. xix.

18. B.P. Hindle, *Medieval Roads and Tracks*, 3rd edn. (Princes Risborough: Shire, 1998), p. 5.

19. Birkholz, *The King's Two Maps*, p. 67.

20. Catherine Delano-Smith suggests there could have been two other regionally-held copies concentrating on geographical locations. Delano-Smith and Kain, *English Maps*, p. 48.

21. Mason, *The Gough Map*, p. 3.

22. Birkholz, *The King's Two Maps*, p. 116.

23. F.M. Stenton, 'The Road System of Medieval England', *Economic History Review* 7 (1936), 1-21, p. 9.

24. R.A. Pelham, 'The Gough Map', *Geographical Journal* 81 (1933), 34-39, p. 35. Pelham cites the work of Sanders, who, concentrating on the Scottish part of the map, dated it as during the time of Edward I due to evidence of bridges (included and excluded), along with the naming of earldoms.

25. The Earldom of Buchan is thought to have been created in 1115 and become dormant in 1340. G.E. Cockayne, *The Complete Peerage of England, Scotland, Ireland, Great Britain, and the United Kingdom, Extant, Extinct, or Dormant*, repr. edn. (Gloucester: Alan Sutton, 1987), pp. 374-376.

26. Birkholz, *The King's Two Maps*, p. 117.

27. Ibid, p. 91.

28. E. Edson and E. Savage-Smith, *Medieval Views of the Cosmos* (Oxford: Bodleian Library, 2004), p. 118.

29. Ranulphi Higden Cestrien, *Polycronicon, 7 libris; cum indice alphabetico, et duplici orbis terrarum descriptione geographica*, British Library, Royal MS. Ms.14.c.IX.

30. Birkholz, *The King's Two Maps*, p. 82.

31. John Ogilby, *Britannia* (London, 1675).

32. *Four Maps of Great Britain Designed by Matthew Paris about A.D. 1250: Reproduced from Three Manuscripts in the British Museum and One at Corpus Christi College, Cambridge* (facsimile), (London: British Museum, 1928).

33. Hindle, *Medieval Roads*, p. 31.

34. Edson and Savage-Smith, *Medieval Views*, p. 32.

35. M.C. Andrews, 'The British Isles on Nautical Charts of the XIVth and XVth centuries', *Geographical Journal* 68 (1926), 474-481, p. 474.

36. Harvey, 'Medieval Maps to 1500', p. 14.

37. Catherine Delano-Smith, in James R. Akerman, *Cartographies of Travel and Navigation* (Chicago and London: University of Chicago Press, 2006), p. 58.

38. Mason, *The Gough Map*, p. 2.

39. Parsons, *Map of Great Britain*, p. 8.

40. Birkholz, *The King's Two Maps*, p. 130.

41. P.D.A. Harvey, 'Local and Regional Cartography in Medieval Europe', in J.B. Harley and David Woodward (eds.), *The History of Cartography*, vol. 1: *Cartography in Prehistoric, Ancient, and Medieval Europe and the Mediterranean* (Chicago and London: University of Chicago Press, 1987), p. 493.

42. Delano-Smith and Kain, *English Maps*, p. 48.

43. Edson and Savage-Smith, *Medieval Views of the Cosmos*, p. 114.

44. Delano-Smith and Kain, p. 8.

45. Vanessa Lawrence, *Harnessing the Power of GIS: Delivering Efficiencies and Improving Effectiveness in the Construction Industry.* Ordnance Survey website (2006) <http://www.ordnancesurvey.co.uk/oswebsite/business/sectors/landproperty/news/articles/powerofgis.html>.

46. Reported in both: F.M. Stenton, 'The Road System of Medieval England'. *Economic History Review* 7 (1936), 1-21, p. 14; and B.P. Hindle, 'Roads and Tracks', in Leonard Cantor (ed.), *The English Medieval Landscape.* (London : Croom Helm, 1982), p. 198.

47. The Gough Map appears as No. 17, 610 in the Summary Catalogue of Western Manuscripts in the Bodleian Library, and its shelfmark is MS. Gough Gen. Top. 16.

48. Parsons, *The Map of Great Britain*, pp. 1-2.

49. Written in another hand in the margin is 'Now in the hands of Mr Gough who has engrav'd it', (itself a reference to James Basire's facsimile published in 1780). These details were kindly supplied by the Society of Antiquaries and appear in: Parsons, *The Map of Great Britain*, p. 1.

50. Parsons, *The Map of Great Britain*, p. 2.

51. Richard Gough, *British Topography. Or, an Historical Account of What has been Done for Illustrating the Topographical Antiquities of Great Britain and Ireland* (London: 1780).

52. Parsons, *The Map of Great Britain*, p. 10.

53. Hindle, 'Roads and Tracks', p. 197.

54. Stenton, 'The Road System of Medieval England', p. 8.

55. Reprinted in Parsons, *The Map of Great Britain*, pp. 16-20.

56. Sir C. Close, 'The Old English Mile', *Geographical Journal* 76 (1930), 338-342, p. 338; J.B.P. Karslake, 'Further Notes on the Old English Mile', *Geographical Journal* 77 (1931), 358-360, p. 358.

57. Hindle, 'Towns and Roads', p. 41.

58. Hindle, 'Roads and Tracks', pp. 198-199.

59. A full statistical analysis has been undertaken by Hindle in 'Towns and Roads', p. 47.

60. Parsons, *The Map of Great Britain*, p. 9.

61. Pelham, 'The Gough Map', p. 38.

62. Although Parsons identified Colgarth as Colwyth, there is no evidence of a place called 'Colwyth' although there is a Colwith in the Lake District. It might be reasonable to assume that we are dealing with Coigach, a remote region to the north of Ullapool.

63. Birkholz, *The King's Two Maps*, p. 124.

64. Ibid., p. 133.

65. This route was not mentioned in Stenton's listing, although Hindle referred to this branch as his Route 2a, noting the intervening distance as 'XX' (repeated in the Appendix of this volume). Hindle, *Medieval Roads*, p. 31.

66. Much of the content in this chapter is a synthesis of the work of Sanders, Parsons and Birkholz, drawing together speculation on certain aspects of the Gough Map's content.

67. Birkholz, *The King's Two Maps*, p. 134.

68. J.R.R. Tolkien and E.V. Gordon, *Sir Gawain and the Green Knight*, 2nd edn., revised by Norman Davis (Oxford: Clarendon Press, 1967). Reproduced by kind permission of Oxford University Press, the Tolkien Estate on behalf of the J.R.R. Tolkien Copyright Trust, and the Estate of Norman Davis.

69. Translation kindly supplied by Samuel Fanous.

70. Geoffrey of Monmouth, *The History of the Kings of Britain*, trans. Lewis Thorpe (Harmondsworth: Penguin, 1966), p. 50.

71. Judith Weiss, *Wace's Roman de Brut. A History of the British. Text and Translation* (Exeter: Exeter University Press, 2006).

72. The sources for the information discussed in this and the following paragraph are footnotes in Parsons, *The Map of Great Britain*.

73. Harvey, 'Local and Regional Cartography', p. 496.

74. Gough, *British Topography*, p. 55.

75. E. Lynam, *British Maps and Map-Makers* (London: Collins, 1944), p. 10.

76. D.J. Price, 'Medieval Land Surveying and Topographical Maps', *Geographical Journal* 121 (1955), pp. 1-10.

77. R.T. Gunther, *Early Science in Oxford*, vol. 2: *Astronomy* (Oxford, 1923), p. 42.

78. J.K. Wright, 'Notes on the Knowledge of Latitude and Longitude in the Middle Ages', *Isis* 13 (1922), 75-98.

79. A fourteenth-century manuscript in the Bodleian Library, MS. Digby 68, gives the following values: Colchester 18° 30', 51° 40' (sic); London 16° 30', 51° 40' (sic); Oxford 15° 0', 51° 50'; Berwick 17° 0', 56° 20'. Latitudes are also given for Canterbury 51° 36', Lincoln 53° 8', Northampton 52° 20' and York 53° 50'.

80. Mason, *The Gough Map*, p. 5.

81. Matthew Paris map of Great Britain in British Library, Cotton MS. Claudius D.,vi, fol. 12v.

82. W.R. Tobler, 'Bidimensional Regression', *Geographical Analysis* 26 (1994), 187-212.

83. Other facsimiles of the map have included those published by James Basire in 1780, the Royal Geographical Society in 1958, and more recently by the Bodleian Library in 1970 and 1998, to accompany the Parsons reprint identifying all place names featured on the map.

84. *Anglia. II Nova tabula* [by Sebastian Münster] (Basileae [Basle]: Apud Henricum Petrum, 1540), British Library Maps C.1.c.2.

85. *Britanniae Insulae quae nunc Angliae et Scotiae regna continent cum Hibernia adjacente nova description, etc.* [with the letters G.L.A., i.e. Georgius Lilius Anglus, after the date], 1546. British Library Maps K.Top.5.1.

86. *Angliae, Scotiae & Hiberniae Nova Description* [by Gerard Mercator]. (Duisburg, 1564).

87. Parsons, *The Map of Great Britain*, p. 14; Daniel Birkholz, 'The Gough Map revisited: Thomas Butler's *The Mape off Ynglonnd, c.1547-1554*', *Imago Mundi* 58 (2006), 23-47.

88. John Ogilby, *Britannia, or, an Illustration of the Kingdom of England and Dominion of Wales by a ... Description of the Principal Roads* (London, 1675).

89. Statement issued in the supporting documentation to the Oxford Digital Library for *The Gough Map – Gateway to Medieval Britain*.

90. The link from the Bodleian Map Room's home page is: <http://www.bodley.ox.ac.uk/guides/maps/herefrme.htm>; there is also a direct link via Queen's: <http://qub.ac.uk/urban_mapping/gough_map>.

91. C.D. Lloyd, and K.D. Lilley, 'Examining Spatial Variation in the Cartographic Veracity of the Gough Map', in G. Priestnall and P. Aplin (eds.), *GISRUK 2006, Proceedings of the GIS Research UK 14th Annual Conference, 5th–7th April 2006 University of Nottingham* (Nottingham: University of Nottingham), 121-125.

List of Illustrations

Further Reading

Birkholz, Daniel, *The King's Two Maps: Cartography and Culture in Thirteenth-century England*. (London: Routledge, 2004).

Birkholz, Daniel, 'The Gough Map Revisited: Thomas Butler's *The Mape off Ynglonnd*, c.1547-1554', *Imago Mundi* 58 (2006), 23-47.

Delano-Smith, Catherine and Roger J.P. Kain, *English Maps: a History* (London: British Library, 1999).

Edson, E. and E. Savage-Smith, *Medieval Views of the Cosmos* (Oxford: Bodleian Library, 2004).

Harvey, P.D.A., 'Local and Regional Cartography in Medieval Europe', in J.B. Harley and David Woodward (eds.), *The History of Cartography*, vol. 1: *Cartography in Prehistoric, Ancient, and Medieval Europe and the Mediterranean* (Chicago and London: University of Chicago Press, 1987), ch. 20.

Harvey, P.D.A., 'Medieval Maps: an Introduction', in J.B. Harley and David Woodward (eds.), *The History of Cartography*, vol. 1: *Cartography in Prehistoric, Ancient, and Medieval Europe and the Mediterranean* (Chicago and London: University of Chicago Press, 1987), ch. 17.

Harvey, P.D.A., 'Medieval Maps to 1500' in Helen Wallis (gen. ed.), *Historians' Guide to Early British Maps*, Royal Historical Society Guides and Handbooks, 18 (London: Royal Historical Society, 1994), ch. 2.

Hindle, B.P., *Maps for Historians* (Chichester: Phillimore, 1998).

Hindle, B.P., *Medieval Roads and Tracks.* 3rd edn. (Princes Risborough: Shire, 1998).

Hindle, B.P., 'Roads and Tracks', in Leonard Cantor (ed.), *The English Medieval Landscape* (London: Croom Helm, 1982), ch. 7.

Hindle, B.P, 'Towns and Roads of The Gough Map (c1360)', *Manchester Geographer* 1 (1980), 35-49.

Lawrence, Vanessa, *Harnessing the Power of GIS: Delivering Efficiencies and Improving Effectiveness in the Construction Industry*, Ordnance Survey website (2006) <http://www.ordnancesurvey.co.uk/oswebsite/business/sectors/landproperty/news/articles/powerofgis.html>

Mason, R., *The Gough Map of Great Britain, 35mm colour filmstrip published by the Bodleian Library, Oxford* (Oxford: Bodleian Library, 1992).

Parsons, E.J.S., *The Map of Great Britain circa A.D. 1360 known as The Gough Map* (Oxford: printed for the Bodleian Library and the Royal Geographical Society by the University Press, 1958).

Parsons, E.J.S., *The Map of Great Britain circa A.D. 1360 known as The Gough Map.* 2nd. edn. (Oxford: Bodleian Library, 1996).

Pelham, R.A., 'The Gough Map', *Geographical Journal* 81 (1933), 34-39.

Sanders, W.B. *The Thirty-second Report of the Deputy Keeper of the Public Records,* 1 (London: HMSO, 1871).

Stenton, F.M., 'The Road System of Medieval England', *Economic History Review,* 7 (1936), 1-21.

Tobler, W.R., 'Bidimensional Regression', *Geographical Analysis,* 26 (1994), 187-212.